# Crow Moon

## reclaiming the wisdom of the dark woods

# Lucy H. Pearce

Womancraft Publishing

Published by Womancraft Publishing, 2024
www.womancraftpublishing.com

ISBN 978-1-910559-88-8
Crow Moon is also available in ebook format: ISBN 978-1-910559-87-1

Typeset: lucentword.com
Cover image and illustrations © Lucy H. Pearce

Womancraft Publishing is committed to sharing powerful new women's voices, through a collaborative publishing process. We are proud to midwife this work, however the story, the experiences and the words are the author's alone. A percentage of Womancraft Publishing profits are invested back into the environment reforesting the tropics (via TreeSisters) and forward into the community.

5% of royalties from this book is shared between the Glenbower Woodland Trust and TreeSisters.

# Praise for Crow Moon

*Powerful, stunning, and transformative writing.*
**Mary Lunnen, author of six books including** *The Powerful Voice*
*of the Quiet Ones* **and** *Your Compass Rose Speaks*

*Like breadcrumbs along the path, Lucy Pearce sprinkles stories, images, and insights about the crow*
*as she leads us deeper into the dark woods of our imagination in search of our authentic selves.*
*This is a book to meditate on and nest in, often. It is filled with the everyday magic of life.*
**Mary Reynolds Thompson, author of** *Reclaiming the Wild Soul* **and**
**the forthcoming** *The Way of the Wild Soul Woman*

*In a similar way to how Clarissa Pinkola Estés revealed to us the magic of the wild wolf, Lucy Pearce*
*and the stories of women in this book bring alive the archetypal Animal Queendom medicine of the*
*Crow an enchanted mirror to show us who we really are and how not to be afraid of the mystery of*
*darkness, so we can heal at a soul level and reconnect to who we were born as, before our conditioning.*
**Nicole Barton, founder of the Archetypal Apothecary Mystery School and host of The Secret Witch Show**

*Crow Moon is a book of talismans. In its polyvocal narrative all singing and cackling together, and*
*in Lucy Pearce's deft weaving, the book is rich with dark, fertile doorways. Crow Moon calls you to*
*the magic of the winged and whispering. Trust that your longing heart will find a home here.*
**Risa Dickens, co-author of** *Missing Witches: Reclaiming True Histories of Feminist Magic*
**and** *New Moon Magic: 13 Anti-Capitalist Tools for Resistance and Re-Enchantment*

*A fascinating, challenging, enchanting flight through the raven-dark*
*heart of the wilds, what it is to be lost and to find oneself.*
**Sarah Robinson, author of** *Yoga for Witches*, *Yin Magic* **and** *Kitchen Witch*

*This book feels like a fever dream, In a good way. In the way that fevers break patterns of pathology and*
*allow the healing crisis to emerge. It reminds me of the health crises of those medieval female mystics.*
*The Hildegards, the Julians, the Teresas of Avila, the Catherines of Sienna, cartographers of the female*
*dark night of the soul. Lucy H. Pearce has drawn us a map, a 21st century GPS, to our essential selves.*
**Gina Martin, author of the** *When She Wakes* **series**

# Also by Lucy H. Pearce

## Books

*The Kitchen Witch Companion: Recipes, Rituals & Reflections* (with Sarah Robinson, Womancraft Publishing, 2023)

*She of the Sea* (Womancraft Publishing, 2021)

*Medicine Woman: reclaiming the soul of healing* (Womancraft Publishing, 2018)

*Full Circle Health: integrated health charting for women* (Womancraft Publishing, 2017)

*Full Circle Health: 3-month charting journal* (Womancraft Publishing, 2017)

*Burning Woman* (Womancraft Publishing, 2016)

*Moon Time: Living in Flow with your Cycle* (Womancraft Publishing, first edition 2015; third edition 2022)

*Reaching for the Moon: a girl's guide to her cycles* (Womancraft Publishing, 2015)

*Moods of Motherhood: the inner journey of mothering* (Womancraft Publishing, 2014)

*The Rainbow Way: cultivating creativity in the midst of motherhood* (Soul Rocks, 2013)

## E-courses

*Be Your Own Publisher*

*Peaceful Patterns*

*Structuring the Soul of Writing*

*WORD+image*

*Your Authentic Voice*

"If you don't go out in the woods nothing will ever happen and your life will never begin."

Clarissa Pinkola Estés

# Crow Moon

Come with me. We'll leave the busy main road behind, where the warm glow of streetlights illuminates the chill evening air. Pull your coat warmly around you and watch your step as we walk downhill into the gloaming. There are loose rocks on the path, and places where the tree roots might catch you unawares.

The woods are quiet. It is just us.

We walk to the bridge over the river. The dark water catches the silver of the rising full moon. The sky turning from pale grey to mauve to pitch black before our eyes.

All is still. And silent.

Our breath makes clouds. Hands dug deep in pockets. Eyes scouring the darkening sky. Hearts beating in our ears.

We wait. Wondering if we are too late.

Too early.

Waiting. Waiting.

Losing faith.

But this is not a moment governed by the clock. It has its own internal timing. A confluence of unseen forces. You must be patient. Stay alert. Your feet grow numb, your senses sharpen.

Then comes the shift. Barely perceptible but nevertheless there.

The dimming light stirs.

Suddenly the sky overhead is alive. From east and southeast, west and northwest, large black birds fly, travelling in their groups of hundreds, swirling, cawing, interweaving, dancing a greeting in the air. The sky is thick black feathered. We watch in awe as they combine and dissipate above our heads, as though we are lying on the bottom of the ocean, looking up at the surface world. Then, without signal or warning, they circle the heart of the wood and land in hidden roosts.

Silence falls once more.

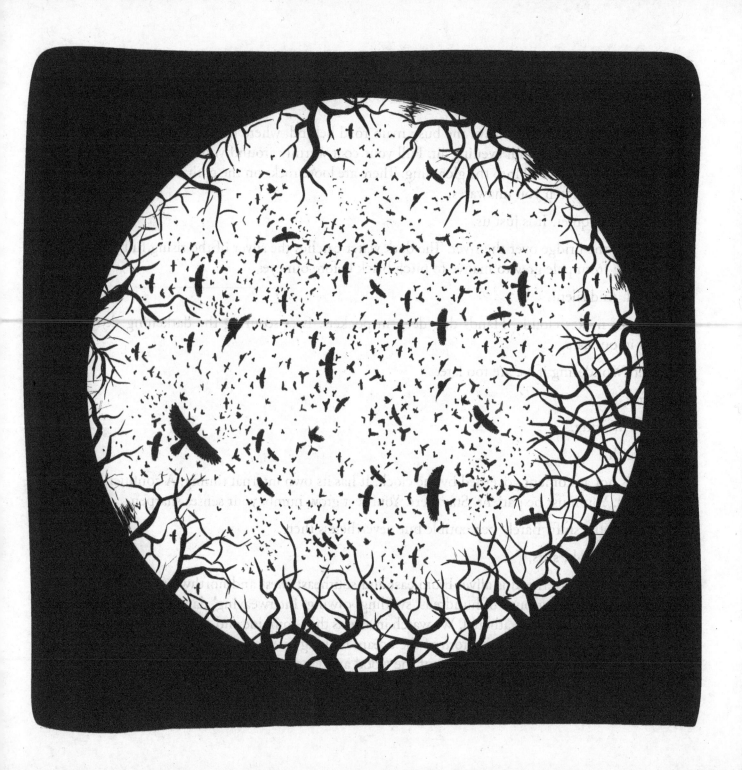

# Lockdown

I have always been fascinated by birds. Always watched them. Sought to know more about them.

As a child I was a member of the Young Ornithologists Club and spent hours of my youth watching them on the bird-feeder, absorbed in their movements, enjoying their company more than that of the noisy children around me. When I was eight, our teacher found a fallen baby jackdaw and we took it in turns to bring it home in a box and feed it with cat food overnight. When I was eleven, we were set a hedgerow project, where we had to observe a hedge for a full year and see what birds and animals came and went, to note how it changed with the seasons.

With young adulthood came study, travel, work and early motherhood in quick succession, and I was too busy navigating the pressing complexities of my own life to stop and watch the birds in open-mouthed wonder and delight.

And then the pandemic hit. The outer world ground to a halt. Busyness evaporated. The streets were empty. We were locked down, our world curtailed. An ominous new order threatened. One that required masks and social distancing, tests and isolation. Death was omnipresent. The future shrouded in bleak uncertainty. The news each day started with the number of deaths, proclaimed by the newsreader in a solemn voice. The world changed in a scary way. Suddenly and all at once, as though a dark dystopian tale had come to life.

We were cut off from friends and family. From most of the things that kept us busy, that gave life pleasure and meaning, that drove us mad and kept us sane.

Simultaneously, in the places where human life once dominated, wildlife began to assert itself. The pictures of a herd of deer trotting down the main street of a small English town and happily grazing on the grass outside an east London housing estate were something I will never forget.[1] It didn't take long before a greater balance was restored: outside and within ourselves. Previously plane-trailed skies were pure blue, humans could no longer fly: we were grounded. The usually quiet woods and car-filled country lanes were full of walkers and the soundtrack to our days was not the endless drone of engines but birdsong, their waking and roosting marking time.

It was a strange time when two futures seemed to co-exist: a dark technological fascist state of checkpoints and vaccine certificates – patriarchy squared – or a future where humans lived smaller lives, more embedded in their local communities, where ecosystems could flourish, where we could co-exist with the wild, where we baked bread, grew vegetables, checked in with each other and really meant it, and lived at a slower, gentler pace. A world where we no longer rushed everywhere but took our time. A world where we could pay attention to the birds, and to everyday magic.

The crows had always been there. They weren't new to me or to our area. In fact, they are probably the bird I see most often: in newly planted fields, rooting in bins next to fast food restaurants, prowling city centre pavements, strutting on beaches, in gardens, perched on the side of the motorway waiting for roadkill, stationed on my chimney pot and calling at five a.m.

Maybe that is it: they are so omnipresent that they become invisible. Hidden in plain sight. So everyday as to be unremarkable.

And so it was entirely by chance that I came across the crows one late afternoon walk on the furthest edges of my five-kilometre lockdown zone. Chaffing my limits, longing for freedom.

One moment I was just walking in the woods.

The next… Crow Moon.

I needed to understand what had just happened.

# Lockdown Reflection

*"In the year of lockdown, I woke one morning to the sound of a soft caw and to see two ravens stripping bark from the she-oak outside my bedroom window. I watched as they flew back and forth with bark, twigs and any fluff they could find to prepare their nest in the tall gum opposite.*

*In that strange and liminal time, this felt like a reminder of what was real, of what really mattered.*

*In my walks around the neighbourhood, I became aware of over a dozen raven nests in just a few suburban blocks. I was suddenly gifted raven feathers in my garden. One was even left on my doorstep. I noticed that the common perception of ravens as aggressive seemed false and that, unlike their corvid cousins the magpie and currawong, the little ravens that thrive in Melbourne were instead quite shy and skittish birds. I watched the gentle intimacy they had with each other and eagerly but unsuccessfully waited to spot the fledglings. I had to wait months before I saw the young families stepping out. Most of the couples had one youngster but 'my' raven couple had two to introduce to the world.*

*I am so grateful for that year of raven magic. I know now that when the first wattles bloom after Winter Solstice that I'll be seeing ravens with beaks full of twigs. I now often dream as Raven, my shoulder blades stretching into wings and my gaze narrowing to pointed focus. That soft caw of a lockdown morning is now woven into the soundscape of home."*

**Linda Ruff**

# A Blessing of Crows

I set about researching what I had observed. The first thing I discovered was that these black birds I had seen in the woods were not in fact crows… but rooks! How had I lived more than forty years not knowing the difference between them?

It is a common mistake to make, it seems. Crows, rooks, ravens and jackdaws are all members of the crow family (*Corvidae*) and live everywhere on the planet except for Antarctica. These medium to large black birds are often interchangeable at a distance (and close-up to the non-expert eye). They tend to be generically referred to as crows, a convention that I will continue in this book. But when I am talking about observations in nature, I will reference the different species.

I learned that crows (in the US) and rooks (in the UK and Ireland where I live) gather together to create winter nesting sites, often in urban woods or parklands, in order to stay safe and warm. Tens of thousands of birds – the largest roost ever recorded in the US had two million birds! – come together from their various feeding patches, many miles away, stopping off at intermediary staging posts along the way to gather in ever-greater numbers on rooftops, treetops and telephone wires. As dusk falls in the coldest months of the year, these groups flock, dancing together in the air and calling noisily before settling into the tall trees to roost for the night. Come first light they disperse once more.

I had instinctively called what I had witnessed a "Crow Moon", and on researching the term learned that in America the full moon in March is called a Crow Moon because the increased activity of crows indicates the arrival of spring. They move to their breeding grounds in smaller groups, courting, noisily gathering nesting materials during the day and building large messy nests in the tallest trees.

Crows appear to the casual gaze to be far cleverer than most other birds – and decades of scientific research has proven that they are. The crow family are considered the most intelligent of the birds: their brain-to-body mass ratio is equal to that of great apes. They are some of the few birds that can learn to mimic human words, phrases and voices as well as the sounds of other animals and even machines.[2] Their desire to observe and engage with human life is quite unusual.

Crows share many behaviours with us: they build strong relationships; they generally mate for life and have been observed mourning the death of another from their group. They also have the ability to play, to recognise individual cars and people, to plan ahead, make and use complex tools, solve

problems, remember those who have hurt or helped them for years, passing on this information to future generations. They often bring gifts to humans who feed them regularly: bones, coins, bottle caps, hair grips, pebbles... [3]

Wherever we have gone, the crows have followed: from our time as hunter gatherers to farmers, feeding from our leftovers and fields. Where we cleared forests and built cities, they gained yet more open territory and new foodstuffs to forage. We have lived in close proximity for all our known history.

In Europe the land is divided between two species of crow – the hooded and carrion crows. But this was not always the case.

Before the last Ice Age, ten thousand years ago, there was a single species of crow in Europe. The encroaching wall of ice forced the crows to seek refuge. Those that headed east evolved into hooded crows, whilst those that went west became carrion crows. [4] The ice sliced neatly between Northern England and Scotland – meaning that even today Scotland and Ireland (along with Scandinavia and Eastern Europe) have hooded crows, with their jet black hoodies and wings and grey bodies, whereas England (and Western Europe) have the all-black carrion crow, It is incredible to think that an event so long ago could have such a long-lasting impact. But it did. There is not an oceanic divide that separates the two species of European crow, simply the imaginal residue of a wall of ice. [5]

In England and Ireland crows tend to be spotted alone or in their breeding pairs, whereas rooks are a highly social bird, hanging out in large groups (as does the American crow).

The rook has a distinctive grey beak with a bald patch of grey skin above it and raggy feathers on its legs. In early September the rooks gather in their hundreds in fields, their sharp beaks drilling the soil for leatherbacks, the larvae of the caddis fly, (often known as daddy-long-legs) which can decimate crops by feeding on their roots when in a larval stage. It is quite a sight, fields carpeted with black birds for a day or two, and then gone.

A gathering of rooks is sometimes called a parliament, and you can see why. They gather as though by pre-arrangement in a field, talking to each other in strange caws.

Some call a group of crows a murder – their presence seen as a bad omen. Other collective nouns include an unkindness of ravens, a clamour of crows, a storytelling of rooks.

I call them a blessing.

A blessing of crows.

# Learning the Woods

The first year after seeing the Crow Moon was a time of childlike wonder and discovery. After years of being called to the shoreline, I headed inland, drawn to the woods and the birds. I set out to learn them by name, beyond my rudimentary childhood knowledge. I learned to differentiate rook from crow, jackdaw from starling, house martin from swallow, by sight and sound.

Guided by apps and friends, books and online groups I learned to see beyond the mass of green and brown, to start to identify more trees by shape and leaf, to make new friends of different species and visit them through the changing seasons.

I began to listen in a different way, beyond the chorus of generic birdsong.

I learned to pick out the tuts and clicks and cackles of the starling,

The melodic waterfall of the robin,

The high-pitched seesaw of the great tit,

The enormous repertoire of the song thrush perched high in the treetops,

The cackle of the magpie,

The caw of the crow.

I added the songs of blue tit, chaffinch, wagtail, wren, goldcrest and chiffchaff to my woodland playlist of favourite artists. Dog walkers would hurry by as I stood rooted to the spot, eyes up, rapt by birdsong: a new dimension of sound which I could not believe I had been so uncurious about before.

I began to walk slower, look closer and soon another new world opened up, this time visually, appearing as though by magic from beneath the leaf litter. A miniature realm filled with the most incredible colours and forms – the world of fungi, which, like the crows, had always been there, hidden in plain sight: stag's horn, Dead Moll's fingers, charcoal bolete, crested coral, fairy parachute, hare's ear, witch's hat…

Their names become mantras to my days, awakening my imagination. I had no interest in the cold Latin names, it was the folk names that spoke to me. The names given by people who saw their shapes and patterns and equivalences in their stories and lives. Jelly ears, velvet soft like the skin of a newborn with the form and structure of a human ear, growing from a rotting tree trunk. Candle-

snuff fungus that looks like the wick of a candle just blown out. Elf cups, tiny red cup forms left in the moss as though the fairy folk had just abandoned a tea party.

Days in the woods became a treasure hunt. Photographing what I found, keeping note of new species, logging their locations to find them again in later years, sharing them eagerly with loved ones and on social media.

When I got home, I often found myself drawing or painting leaves and trees and of course the Crow Moon. With practice I grasped the ability to recreate a visual verisimilitude in pencil, water-colour and ink.

But something was missing.

Something else.

# A Crow in the Family

*"I grew up in and now live in rural New South Wales, Australia where crows are seen as evil and predatory. My first memory of Crow was hearing my uncle complain about them killing lambs and blinding the older ewes. That coloured my thinking a lot as a young person.*

*I started paying attention to Crow when my ninety-year-old nan blurted out at a family dinner, that my great-grandmother, Nellie, told her she was coming back as a crow when she died. I thought if Nellie was coming back as a crow, then they probably weren't that bad. I was in my late twenties by then.*

*Since then, I have seen Crow at pivotal moments of my life – one memory that stands out was when my husband and I lived in Scotland, on a tiny island off the Isle of Skye.*

*One year at the end of summer, a huge crow appeared outside my office window. For almost an entire week, I would watch this crow swoop in and out of the paddock. It was odd enough that my workmates and I talked about it.*

*On the Saturday night of that week, I received a phone call from Australia telling me my grandfather had died. Crow wasn't there the next day – I know because I sat in front of that paddock all day, grieving and writing.*

*Exactly one year later, Crow reappeared. Swooping in and out of the same field. It was noticeable and again in the office we talked about the crow, wondering if it was the same one as last year. For almost a week the crow was there, until my friend and work colleague received a call that her grandmother had died. Crow wasn't there the next day. And we were all very relieved that Crow wasn't there the next year.*

*Today sometimes I don't see Crow, but she will leave me a gift of one of her beautiful feathers. She gives me great comfort because when I see her, I know that I am on the right track I just need to lean into the harder parts, but I am not alone. And when I see Crow, I meet her by saying 'Hello Nellie.'"*

**Kirstin McCulloch**

"Crows have always held a special place in my heart. I cannot pinpoint when or why it started, but for as long as I can remember, since I was a little girl [...] they have fascinated me. It may be because when I look into their eyes, I get a distinct feeling that they know something so much more significant than I could ever comprehend, something other-worldly."

M.J. Cullinane, *Crow Tarot*

# Something Else

Understanding the what, why and how of the crows and their seasonal gathering only got me so far. Millions of people each day live in the vicinity of roosting birds, and they barely register it. Their lives are not tilted on their axis from the experience of seeing them. They do not find themselves suddenly obsessed by these birds and the woods they call home. I will give some allowance for my neurodivergent brain – crows have most certainly become a special interest, I take great joy in finding out as much as I can about them, reading books, joining Facebook groups of thousands of people who are also fascinated by these birds…

But there was something else too.

Something about the experience that I could not put into words, but longed to express. Something about the way I stood entranced, enchanted by this moment that was both happening in reality and yet seemed to shift my consciousness, so that I was both there and somewhere else, simultaneously. It felt momentous. Important. As though I was being literally touched by the experience, as though there was some sort of mystical exchange or communication happening. I was transformed and transported. And yet, to the outside world it seemed insignificant. I was just a woman, standing in the wood, watching birds doing what they do.

At the time I first saw the Crow Moon I was editing Molly Remer's book, *Walking with Persephone*. In it she writes of crows as messengers. She writes:

"The sound or sight of a crow is always a sign for me to stop and pay attention – it becomes a self-reinforcing encounter with everyday magic. The crow is a trigger for me – listen, watch, look here, reflect, think, feel, experience, *be here right now*. And in so stopping, I often see or experience something magical, surprising, or significant. Whether or not magic is there already (out of my awareness) or it is merely the simple association with the crow as a sign to pay attention which causes me to look more closely and to develop associations, make connections, or notice symbols and make significance out of the mundane world, the end result is the same – I pause, notice, encounter, and experience, and the encounter itself *becomes magic* in that act of noticing and experiencing."

This was what I had experienced. This is what I longed for more of. I decided to pay attention to the crows, and to keep seeking out the magic of the woods… and that place, that feeling in myself.

OOO

I experienced the same sensation again a year later at Samhain, as we joined a Halloween lantern procession. Dozens of us carried lanterns through the darkening woods, as the birds came in to roost. We were led by a group of drummers and a woman in a long black coat, top hat and a beaked mask – the mask of the plague doctor of old, relevant once more in these modern plague times. I wore a black hooded cape that I had bought for my daughter's school play, but had secretly wanted myself.

There was something about this cape, the crows, the wild rhythm of the drums, the ancient ritual of going into the forest, of celebrating the darkening season. It connected to the experience in the woods the year before, that I had started to refer to as a Crow Moon. There was something deeply exciting. Something I was longing for. Something I didn't get to experience very often in my daily life. Something primal. Something vital.

I felt bigger. More alive. More myself.

There was that feeling again: magical and real. Both, simultaneously.

The sense of being in an experience that was multi-layered. Something that was happening here in the world, and yet seemed to have other dimensions. Something outside of me was mirroring something within, in a strange unseeable dance.

That night I could not go to sleep. I reached for my new iPad (a brave gift I had requested to support my creativity, something that intuitively felt like the next step, yet at the same time too much to ask for). I picked it up and began to draw in the dark.

The picture of a caped woman emerged quickly in a style I had not used before. In black and white. This image. This style. The ease with which it emerged intrigued me. There was no thought or planning.

I came back to this image, day after day. Curious about it. And yet... it also scared me.

Who was this? Why did they appear? Why now?

OOO

Something within me was hungry to follow the image and the feelings it evoked in me.

Something in these experiences in the woods was enlivening something deep within me. Something beyond logic or basic emotion. The part of me that I have learned to call soul or psyche.[6]

# Both/And

Though this book starts with a very real Crow Moon, I must warn you now that it is not a book about crows. Or moons. Not in the way you may be expecting. Although both feature heavily.

I think it's best to clear that up right now.

OOO

Look at a crow… What do you see?

A black bird: sharp beak, clawed feet, dark feathers with an iridescence in some lights and a beady eye. Look closer and you may now recognise it as an individual species of the Corvid family – rook, crow or raven. Spend longer and you may in time come to recognise this individual's unique behaviours and physical characteristics that distinguish it. You may learn its territory and nesting site. You may watch it nest in spring and come in to roost at dusk.

This is the physical crow, studied by biologists and behaviourists. But look again, there is more that we see when we see a crow. Much more.

We see what Crow[7] *means* to us, not only as individuals from our personal experience, but what Crow has meant to our culture and to humans across cultures – philosophically, spiritually, emotionally. We are aware of what Crow *symbolises*.

The crows that you will come across in this book are real… *and* symbolic.

Both/and.

# The Symbol Makers

Since the beginning of human history, animals of all sorts have meant something to us on a symbolic level, beyond merely being fellow creatures, food, foe, producers of useful resources, companions and helpmeets. We have observed them and ascribed to them certain characteristics, human emotions and meanings in our art, stories and religions. We have also, across cultures, chosen to create symbolic powerful hybrid creatures part-human, part-animal. Over our history as a species, we have understood that there was some sort of innate connection between us and other animals: we have understood our stories, our origins and our fates as indelibly intertwined.

Humans have instinctively used images or words to not only communicate an animal's literal meaning but also a deeper symbolic meaning. Our use of symbol creates a bridge between the physical and the non-physical (psychic) worlds, between our inner and outer worlds. Over time a symbol used by many members of a society becomes loaded with cultural meaning and is used as shorthand in art, stories and rituals.

Religion and art both draw on the same symbol-making faculty in order to express the inexpressible, employing metaphor to speak for the far reaches of human experience, attempting to communicate that which is deeply known, but always lies just out of sight.

Birds and symbols of birds have often represented qualities that we have longed for. They have captivated us with their ability to fly, unlike us earthbound creatures. Birds in flight have represented ideas of freedom, joy and transcendence. The human soul or spirit is often depicted as a bird, something which is caged in the body during our lifetimes, but flies free briefly during dreams and visions and permanently at death.

For millennia across human cultures birds have been seen as conduits between god(s) and humans, between the realms of sky and land, not quite belonging to either, passing with ease between both. Birds' behaviour and appearances have been used to foretell the future, a form of divination known as augury. Even today the sudden appearance of a murder of crows in a field, a single magpie ("one for sorrow, two for joy") flying in front of our car, seems to hold weight... it seems to mean something.

"Man, with his symbol-making propensity, unconsciously transforms objects or forms into symbols (thereby endowing them with great psychological importance) and expresses them in both his religion and his visual art. The intertwined history of religion and art, reaching back to prehistoric times, is the record that our ancestors have left of the symbols that were meaningful and moving to them."

Aniela Jaffé, *Man and his Symbols*

# Crow as Symbol

Crows with their intelligence, curiosity and opportunism have sparked the human imagination across time and culture: featuring in a hundred thousand songs, stories, costumes, drawings, paintings, poems, myths and legends around the world. They mean something to us. Something deep and untouchable.

Crows are depicted in the cave paintings of Lascaux, France – both attending the hunt and as a strange half-bird half-man figure: medicine man, god, chieftain, hunter, dreamer? A collection of crow feathers was discovered with a Neanderthal body: objects that are buried with a body, in any culture, either mark a person's earthly status, or an offering to help their passage to the next life. They give us a clue to what was valued, and what their beliefs around death were.

Far, far back at the dawn of humanity we have evidence of Crow emerging as both a valued companion and an important symbol: Crow as shapeshifter, Crow as connected to death, Crow as guide.

Crow has appeared consistently as a symbol throughout arts and cultures, variously representing the soul, the trickster, the goddess, a trusted carrier of messages between gods and men. They are seen as a mediating force between this world and the Otherworld, between the realms of Earth and Air, heaven and earth, life and death. In Scotland, the hooded crow is associated with the fairy realm. In Welsh mythology, witches and magicians could transform into crows or ravens to avoid being captured. In Norse mythology, Thought and Memory are depicted in raven form, wise companions to the great god Odin. In Celtic mythology, the triple goddess Morrigan/Badb takes winged form as a crow who appears on the battlefield. In the Bible, the raven is the first to be sent to find dry land after the flood, he comes back empty-beaked, it is the white dove that brings the olive branch and with it hope.

"Crows are ministers of veiled mysteries. [...] Like dark angels come to set the balance of the natural order to rights. [...] We never grasp the full measure of the birds. They subvert our attempts to do so, just as the tricksters, magicians and cultural heroes they embody in folklore and myth subvert our fondest notions of human superiority, put in question what constitutes the reality of sacred or profane. [...] The crow or raven daemon perched on our psyches open doors, steal treasures for us from hidden places, coax us out of our narrow, conventional shells – and also mercilessly confuses us."

*The Book of Symbols*

# Shifting Meanings

Every time we see a crow, we see not only their embodied reality, but the layers upon layers of symbology that we are aware of from visual art, myth, poetry and folk tales of what Crow *means*.

But this meaning is not static. It has changed over the course of history, most markedly in European culture, a transformation that has had significant impact on both the lives of real crows, and on us.

Crow moved from ally – spiritual messenger of the gods and practical assistant cleaning up the carcasses of our hunting trips – to being perceived not only as an agricultural pest – vying for an unwarranted share of the crops – but also a public nuisance – pecking on the dead bodies of plague victims and the charred bodies of the Great Fire of London. At the very beginning of the early Enlightenment era, as the roots of the rationalist culture we inhabit today were becoming firmly established, crows were legislated against across Europe. They were hunted, stoned, shot into submission.

European colonists brought these practices to America, the land of Native Crow tribes, with Crow languages, and the revered trickster Crow depicted on totem poles. It is no surprise that these Europeans who dreamed of spiritual purity and transcendence of death would scorn the unsettling black bird long associated with death and the nature gods of their ancestors.

The God of the Bible was not one who spoke in the voice of animals. To use the movements of birds to foretell the future flew in the face of Christian beliefs. And in time crows became associated with the human ministers of evil and death: witches. In folklore, witches were frequently depicted as either having a crow as a pet or familiar, or said to be able to shapeshift into one.

The crow and the witch became connected in the mainstream imagination as the enemy of the good, to be hunted down and eradicated. In the world of the priest, the plague doctor, the huntsman, the farmer, the king and the hangman: the crow and the witch and all they stood for, were not to be tolerated. Good Christians were instructed by the word of God not to suffer a witch to live.

And so, the persecution of witches and crows became an entangled fight against the darkness, the irrational, the uncontrollable, the wild, death…against forces that were threatening to patriarchal dominance and control.

This discomfort in the Western world around crows – and witches – exists to this day. There is something about them that unsettles us still. Something we cannot quite put our finger on. Some-

"Concepts of good and evil arose with agriculture, when humans began to expunge the weeds and the wolves, and to spread domesticity across the land. No longer were we part of the wild; separate from us, the wild became first a concept and then an enemy. Evil became associated with chaos, good with order. Accordingly, the idea of progress arose as well. It was the destiny of humankind to become lords and masters of nature, to subdue its cruelty with kindness, its chaos with predictability and security. In the last few centuries, we have dreamed of completing this conquest: leaving nature behind altogether to ascend into space."

Charles Eisenstein, "Handfuls of Dust"

thing discomforting. Eerie. Scary even.

But still they endure.

Still, they thrive.

In the shadows. In the dark woods.

Reminding us of death and chaos.

## At home today as always

*"The crow perches as proudly upon the prongs of a satellite dish, as it does upon the branches of ash, digesting a new image of the world but remaining holy black, as it always has, under the low sun.*

*The crow is so at home in this time and yet it has been here for such a long time. As black as the unconsciousness of our lives and yet able to sit with the shifting, always seeing."*

**Holly Baker**

# Crow as Omen

This dual nature of Crow – powerful in terms of both good and ill – is seen in its developing symbology over the past centuries. For some Crow is used as an identity and symbol of power, luck or protection on coats of arms, sports team mascots and by Native tribes: the blessing of crows. They have also, however, been associated with portents, omens and foretellings, usually of the dark or scary kind, partly because of their colour: black being associated in many cultures with death. But also because of where they are found. Crows are scavengers, and so were often to be found on the battlefield, in cemeteries and execution sites, pecking at bodies.

These powerful birds have guarded the Tower of London – the site of royal executions for centuries – since the seventeenth century after King Charles II was warned that if the six ravens in residence at the Tower left, England would fall. Still today there is a royal command that there must be six ravens present at the Tower at all times. They even have their own keeper there – The Ravenmaster – who feeds them and trims their wings to ensure they stay.

On January 13th 2021, as I wrote this book, the raven known as "the Queen of the Tower" died, bringing the number of birds at the Tower to just seven, the lowest it has been for many years.[8] In 2022 Queen Elizabeth, the longest reigning monarch in British history, died and England cycled through three Prime Ministers in almost as many months, the economy nosedived… coincidence or a sign of the power of the prophecy?

…

One of the woods I walk in, Rostellan Woods, was the subject of a similar crow-related prophecy.

The story goes that William O'Brien, the 4th Earl of Inchiquin, wanted to build a grand house for his new bride. The site he picked was a former graveyard by the lake in Rostellan, County Cork. He ordered that the graves be levelled and set about building. A local woman whose only son was buried in the graveyard pleaded with him to abort his plans. When he refused, she cursed him, saying that his line would die out because of his actions. Furthermore, she warned, whilst his family lived in Rostellan no rooks would roost there. There would be no blessing of crows for the O'Brien family.

At the time of the curse the Earl was a wealthy man with four daughters and four sons. Within thirty years every one of his heirs, bar a daughter who could neither speak nor hear, was dead.[9] The palatial house now lies in ruins.

It has been reclaimed by the community and the wild: families walk dogs through the arches and rubble, children make dens and rope swings in the trees that grow in the old walled kitchen garden, teenagers drink beer in the abandoned icehouse, adrenaline junkies ride mountain bikes around its dirt tracks and foragers gather mushrooms. It is a place teeming with life: plant, fungal, bird and animal.

But over three hundred years later the rooks still do not roost there.

## The Foretelling

*"One day, when I was living alone on a mountain, hundreds of crows moved onto my large property and stayed for days. It was an utter marvel. Suddenly I had a medical event and was rushed to a hospital where I nearly lost my life. Six days later, I came back to my mountain home and the crows were still there. They stayed for a couple more days, then they all together moved on. I felt they knew of my possible immanent death and came in to surround me with their energy. As I stabilized, they weren't needed any more and off they went."*

**Tayria Ward**

# Crow Today

Today the crow has a mixed reputation within mainstream European and colonial cultures. One of our most common birds, it is ignored by most, unremarked on for its appearance or song, and seen as a pest by many farmers and householders.

However, in many Indigenous cultures as well as in contemporary pagan, witch and alternative spirituality circles, the crow is considered to be a symbol of great significance and importance, often referred to as crow medicine, and celebrated as a totem or spirit animal.

*"In Glastonbury crows are referred to as the Nine Morgan Sisters, and I call on these Sisters for my own healing for they know the unseen untameable world that surrounds me and also that lives within me. These wonderful elemental beings remind me of my primal natural self, remembering when I was able to fly, way back in my evolutionary memory. Tuning into my breath I become one with the wind, the lightning, with the thunderous rage that rumbles around in my own inner landscape and then I become the sky reaching down in ecstatic embrace of the earth.*

*Crow medicine is the ability to transform a deep longing or loss into life again, to be reminded that we are all a part of an intricate web of life, where life lives on, with and through life in all Her manifestations. Crow medicine is not for everyone, but is gifted to anyone who is in need. Crow reminds me that I can place a foot in each world, that I can live this life remembering I am a soul within a human body, shapeshifting through my human existence, where I can wear my cloak of black feathers and commune with the very essence of this Mother World, deeply connected in the love and grace that is here."*

**Susie Quatermass**

*"Crow is one of my spirit guides, and a messenger. She shows up when I need to either pay attention to a message I am about to receive or to explore deeper into something I am currently working on. She reminds me to connect to my higher self and my shadow side."*

**Kirstin McCulloch**

*"Crow represents a message from the divine. It can be connected to change and transformation. As spirit animals they represent:*

*- Higher perspective*

*- Fearlessness*

*- The mystery of creation*

*- Personal transformation*

*- Magic and destiny*

*The message I hear is:*

*- Change is coming*

*- Tap into your higher self*

*- Do not be afraid of your darkness (it is an opportunity to learn)*

*- Follow your path (you will be guided)."*

**Christina Swan-Doyle**

*"Crows represent conviction, choosing a path less trodden, they are a symbol of perseverance through it all, and connection to wisdom and spirit."*

**Rebecca Kimberley**

*"The crow is a strong goddess symbol, reconnecting us with the Wise Woman. She flies and navigates between the realms, reminding us of change, transformation and integrating all aspects of being, including the shadow parts."*

**Reva Adie**

## Soul Guide

*"I first became aware of crows as soul guides in a dream about thirty years ago. Life as I knew it was about to come completely undone. I could sense it but did not yet have the information about what was going on that was destined to blow everything apart. In my dream, I was in an open field with a forest nearby. A crow flew by, and I knew to follow it. I ran after it as it joined its flock who were flying just at the edge of the forest. I felt they had called me and were leading me. I ran after them with great energy and trust. I have never forgotten this dream; it is completely numinous to me still.*

*My life did blow up. And the crows kept showing up for me, in waking life and in dreams, always giving me a deep sense of their magic and mystery, helping me feel not alone as I navigated the dissolution."*

**Tayria Ward**

# The Dark Woods

Just as with the crows, the woods in this book both are – and are not – real forests of pine and cedar, oak and ash trees.

*Crow Moon* is not only about our adventures in the outer woods, but the trek through the shadowy places within ourselves to encounter the unknown or rejected aspects of self.

"Since ancient times the near impenetrable forest in which we get lost has symbolized the dark, hidden, near-impenetrable world of our unconscious."[10]

In the thirteenth century Dante wrote in his *Divine Comedy* of the dark woods:

"In the middle of the journey of life, I came to myself, in a dark wood, where the direct way was lost. It is a hard thing to speak of, how wild, harsh and impenetrable that wood was."

The dark wood is a powerful metaphor we instinctively understand both from lived experience and cultural narratives, most commonly myths and fairy tales. Being lost in a dark wood speaks to the sense of bewilderment and confusion that we experience, and the corresponding inner experience of trying to navigate internally when we have lost our bearings.

This encounter with the dark forest within tends to happen at moments of immense inner and outer change, most commonly in the transition of midlife, or at any time of the death of a significant person in our lives. The self we once thought ourselves to be no longer functions as it once did. We often find that we neither recognise the person we have become nor the roles we are inhabiting. This sense of inner dislocation often seems reflected in the world beyond our bodies. In the wise words of interfaith minister and spiritual counsellor Reverend Dr Sushmita Mukherjee:

"This dark forest is indeed an encounter with the end of a phase of life, and an invitation to [...] what Jung called "individuation" – the integration of opposites – of no longer shoving things we didn't like into the unconscious, and/or projecting it on to other people. [...] Until we enter the dark forest and lose the straight path ahead, we can be assured that we have been traveling the communal path, the path chosen for us by our family, our teachers, our institutions, our society. But as we enter this dark forest – we are finally confronted with the potential of our own unique selves. Our very own flavor, our very own color, our very own taste. To the extent that we are able to then find our path out of this dark forest – through its many false turns and hidden snags and snares – we start to become truly ourselves."[11]

Darkness has consistently been a place of danger and fear for humans – our strongest sense is our sight; in darkness this is disabled. But in European culture darkness has taken on a symbolic meaning – it has been associated with chaos and evil. The aim of Western cultures has been illuminating the darkness, literally (through the technology of the day), psychologically (through reason – the light of the mind), socially (through colonising darker races), and spiritually (through walking into the light of the one true God of patriarchy).

The journey to the dark woods to reclaim the rejected parts of ourselves is one little understood or encouraged within patriarchy, as it is an undertaking that cannot be rationalised or controlled. This unseen process threatens the sense of order and control so valued by the patriarchy, both in the disruption of the individual's supposedly solid and immutable persona and their ability to function economically, but also the potential social repercussions of this chaos.

When we think of forests, we tend to focus on their primary visual components: the trees.

Symbolically, the tree is often used to represent "the growth and development of psychic life (as distinct from instinctive life, commonly symbolized by animals)."[12] The symbol of the Tree of Life is found in many cultures, often to represent a blueprint for a tripartite way of being equally balanced between three realms – rooted in the Underworld, a strong trunk in the Middle or daily world and branches reaching to the heavens or Higher realms. The mirroring of roots and branches, its longevity and ability to weather droughts and storms, and in temperate climes its changing seasonal appearance has made the tree a go-to metaphor for how a wise and grounded person should live.

"As a symbol of rebirth, [the cosmic tree] recalls the human nervous system. Its trunk is the base of the spine, where the cobra of earth energy lies coiled – very like the energy Hindu philosophers call the *kundalini*."

Layne Redmond,
*When the Drummers Were Women*

Biologically speaking there is an unseen layer to the forest: the mycelial layer. This realm of microscopic fungal threads below the forest floor connects tree roots, carrying electrical impulses and nutrients in a vast web of interbeing. When thinking of the psyche it corresponds to a yet deeper layer of the unconscious – the collective unconscious.

The only evidence of this unseen world beneath, to us surface-dwelling humans, is the annual emergence of weird and wonderful mushroom bodies. As we learn to navigate the dark woods, we become aware of this magical kingdom. Once thought to be part of the plant kingdom, in recent years fungi have been given their own classification, being closer genetically to us as humans than to any plant (a strange fact which thrills me to the core).

Fungi, like crows, feed off the dead and dying, acting as a vital part of the cycle of life, an aspect that often disgusts or scares us. The edge that fungi inhabit is that between the surface and the Underworld, a realm often associated with death and evil. Like Crow, fungi also take the form of Trickster – with many species being easily mistaken to the uninitiated – they can feed or poison, heal or harm.

Mushrooms have had connections to the Otherworld throughout history. As with Crow, they are associated with witches, elves and fairies. Their Irish name means 'appearing overnight' and many species grow in magical-seeming circular formations known as fairy rings, places where it was believed fairies would gather.

Agents of transformation, fungi both fascinate and scare our culture with an incredible diversity of otherworldly forms that mimic other species or seem too alien to belong here on Earth. Consuming certain mushrooms can produce visions, enabling people to see and speak with the gods. With these strange forms, mind-altering properties and sudden appearances, it is little wonder they became associated with magic, witches and evil and therefore rejected by patriarchal culture.

# Warning

This is both
A book
And a portal to a place
Within/without.
A wild place.
A strange place.
A magical place.
The dark woods
You may have avoided
All your life.
This is a book about you, and me, and what happens
When we leave the well-trodden path
And the stories of the world
And who we are
Behind us
When we follow the crow and the mushroom
And walk into the dark woods
Under the light of the moon.
The woods are a dangerous place for those who want to stay the same.
But for those in search of adventure, new discoveries, transformation;
for those seeking powerful women, strange gods, animal helpers, plant
allies and feathered goddesses – the dark woods are calling.

Every forest has a secret or two.

Just below the surface.

Hidden beneath the ferns.

An abandoned building disappearing under gnarled roots.

A body sequestered beneath the soil.

Strange calls in the night.

Mysterious creatures slinking unseen in the shadows.

Buried treasure...

A prophecy...

A gift...

Waiting to be discovered

By those who are willing to search.

Here in the paradox of becoming,

you will lose your bearings.

What is becomes what is not.

You may get lost in the woods.

That is the point.

Do not lose yourself.

(You will lose yourself).

# The Wild Soul

The psyche speaks in images and symbols. Images that emerge from the dark unseen wellspring within. Images that seep from the collective unconscious. Images that find us through books and art and film. Images that haunt our minds during the day and dreams during the night, that appear constantly in the world around us. Images that cross our paths in the form of animals and plants and fungi in our daily world.

These are the images to pay attention to.

These are the soul writ large in the world, calling to us.

Symbolic images are an invitation to another way of being in the world. A deeper form of communion. One where the boundaries of inner and outer fall away and something larger, more magnificent, opens up.

We do not make up these symbols. Instead, they appear, fully formed, in our mind's eye, on the page before us, in a forest glade: communications from a mysterious beyond.

This can be strange. Discomforting. It does not align with the way we were taught the world works.

There are many lies at the heart of our modern Western culture which are passed off as truths: that we understand the mechanics of the world; that our purpose as humans is to work and care and earn; that our daily lives are devoid of any deeper meaning.

But our human longing for meaning did not go extinct with the declaration of post-modernism.

We have not out-evolved the mythopoetic.

Revelation did not stop five hundred years ago.

The symbols which have erupted in the consciousness of every generation of humans and have been expressed in art, music, religion since the dawn of our history have not disappeared.

They are still there – inside, outside – waiting for us to discover them anew.

Our basic human drive to connect with something greater than ourselves is still there, numbed by the busyness and distractions and stresses of daily life, beyond the bright screens of our phones churning out endless narratives and empty images. We are longing for intimacy with what lies beyond… and within.

"Create a clearing in the dense forest of your life and wait there patiently until the song that is your life falls into your own cupped hands and you recognise and greet it. Only then will you know how to give yourself to your life so worthy of you."

Martha Postlewaite

The soul hungers for magic and to make meaning in the midst of the mundane.

It finds symbol and metaphor in the dirt and dark corners of the daily, and works with them to transform itself. If we allow it.

"A true symbol appears only when there is a need to express what thought cannot think or what is only divined or felt."

Aniela Jaffé, *Man and his Symbols*

It insists that there is more, far more, to life than what lies on the surface. And that in the wild places magic still lives and the sacred speaks to every one of us, in many different voices. If only we will slow down and listen.

The wild and its ways have been little wanted in the patriarchal project. They have been demonised, sanitised, feared and tamed for generations. The wild may so scare us that we cut ourselves off from it. Within and without.

When we are busy in our domestic and work lives, we tend to overlook the dark and strange world of the psyche. The soul remains underground, out of sight. Until it emerges at last, seeking out wildness.

Our wild nature within and wild nature outside of us are reaching out for each other like long-parted lovers, hungry to intermingle, to be as one once more. The sacred within us is drawn to the sacred beyond, longing for co-existence.

The wild asserts itself, erupting through the cracks in the pavement of our perfectly manicured lives, sending out roots and shoots in the midst of suburbia, trying to rewild the world and ourselves, grabbing our attention through the crumbling of our worldly selves, finances, relationships, health…

When the narrative of our lives comes apart at the seams, the wild chaos at the heart of all things breaks through and insists that we pay attention to the wildness at the heart of a world we thought we had mastered.

# Crow in the Car Park

*"My connection with Crow started in the most unlikely of places. Grimy inner city trading estate at dawn… leftover food wrappings pecked by inquisitive beaks. Black feathers glistening, like the diesel leaks littering the carpark.*

*In the months following my mum's death, the gym became my salvation. Waiting for it to open so I could process the grief, by moving it through my body. I don't feel like I'd ever really seen a crow until we shared that same space in the grimy carpark. It felt like they were all looking at me… but really, they were looking out for me.*

*Without much thought, I was soon joking that the crows were like the old crow I'd lost… my mum, coming to keep an eye on me. However, I soon realised that Crow was always there when I felt alone. Flying alongside and above my car. Appearing when I needed guidance or comfort. Calling out to me in the metaphorical darkness. Always there to say hello.*

*Many years later, after breakups and breakdowns, I found myself on pilgrimage to Glastonbury. Following a magickal dip in the white springs, I distanced myself from the group as we walked back to where we were staying. I felt Crow nearby and spotted them sitting on a rooftop. I watched while they preened and cawed, and saw one of them pulling a fluffy feather from its belly. I gazed in wonder as it drifted on the breeze and daydreamed that it would land right in front of me. As it drifted closer, I realised it was coming straight for me and as I held out my hands, the feather gently landed in them. My heart exploded with overwhelming love. It felt like an initiation and a belonging.*

*I also met the Morrigan that weekend, showing herself in my dreams, in symbology and synchronicities.*

*Now, I live in union with Morrigan and her crows. They come in moments to shift time to a more magickal place. Slowing the clock and making the world appear as though for my eyes only. It's there I find clarity and hear the voice of my soul. Magickal Crow… always guiding me as I thrive, always there to greet me when I arrive… reminding me that I'm alive."*

Eva Lake

# Nature/Reality

We learn the world in dualities: something is either this or that, material or immaterial, natural or supernatural, me or other…

Yet the nature of reality and the reality of nature is staggeringly complex, multilayered and – dare I say it – irrational. Most of it doesn't make logical sense to the mind: it is nuanced, paradoxical, contradictory, rich and strange. Yet there it is: our everyday setting. So we try to understand it using the frames of reference our era offers us: primarily science and evidence-based rationalism, as well as religion and perhaps folklore and mythology… Those parts that we can't make sense of using these frameworks, we ignore and file away with all the other scraps of reality that we do not comprehend. We do our best to spend our lives inhabiting the spaces that feel familiar, safe and known, and avoiding those that are too strange or inexplicable to us. We do the same with ourselves: cutting off, ignoring, denying the parts that do not fit into the prevailing world view.

That does not mean that they do not exist.

In order to understand the world better and come to terms with it, we have woven stories around it, to help ourselves feel safe. And in these narratives, we create a role for ourselves and our relationships to all things that we encounter. Our story of ourselves is tied to our stories of reality.

In time these narrative frameworks become the lens through which we then perceive the world. They become our worldview. In time we do not see the world as it is, but as we have been taught it is. We no longer touch the livingness at the heart of all things. And it no longer touches us.

And so we find ourselves walking through the world, headphones on, with a head full of stories and morphing shadows, not actually experiencing reality as it is.

For most of our history, human cultures have acknowledged that we inhabit a world full of mystery. A living world where death was always present at the heart of life. A world of inexplicable synchronicities. A world interwoven with supernatural entities, gods and spirits. A world rich in meaning.

But in the modern Western world we are taught from a young age to prioritise a scientific, human-centric narrative above all else: a lens that deadens, distorts and simplifies the natural world and our relationship to it, physically and intellectually detaching us from it, insisting that we are separate autonomous agents. Just as religion has become about faith in a dogma long codified by men of power, rather than a direct, active revelationary experience of the sacred in ourselves and the world. In time we learn to distrust or be disinterested in both our biological selves and the deep inner life

of the soul, becoming hypnotised by the surface life we have been taught to value.

Any experiences that don't correlate with this surface reality as we have been taught, we disregard. Ignoring the inconsistencies. Distrusting our instincts.

But there are certain points when the stories that have held us break down and we find ourselves alone in the woods, inner or outer. The old maps cannot guide us, and the old stories begin to fall away.

It is at these times, when we are lost and the light is failing, that the crows might find us.

"Everything has a secret soul that is
silent more often than it speaks."

Kandinsky

# Fear and Becoming

*"The day my beloved horse left us, a raven circled over our heads as I walked her round the field for the last time. "It's time," the throaty croak seemed to say. 'Time for what?' I wondered.*

*Perhaps I should go back. Back to when ravens first started to make appearances in my life. They came in dreams at first. And then I began to hear their calls. I would watch them soaring and swooping as they saw off the juvenile buzzards in the area. But there was one day when Raven really flew into my life. I had left the institutional church some years before and had been gingerly finding my way along a path of nature-based spirituality. I say gingerly because although I was relieved to be free the homophobic and misogynistic environment that I had found so constraining, I was discovering that the old evangelical attitudes and teaching had become deeply rooted in my psyche and soul. Like a plant with deep tap roots, they popped up when I was trying to enter new territory, holding me back and barring my way.*

*"Does anyone know anything about the significance of ravens?" My question was asked tentatively. I was attending one of my first Equine-facilitated workshops. The corvids had been showing up more frequently. I had recently been introduced to shamanic journeying and although part of me was afraid, I was feeling drawn. I was still finding my way and discovering that even though intellectually I could profess a change of belief, the fact was that terror would rise up as I tried to move into a different experience of the sacred.*

*That morning, driving to the hill farm in Wales, I felt sick with anxiety. The previous day there had been discussions of experiences that my old churches would have labelled pagan or even demonic. I made a heartfelt prayer as we drove up a hillside shrouded in early morning autumn mist. As the words were still echoing in my heart the mist began to clear, swirling and dissipating to reveal a landscape full of autumnal hues. "If you asked for bread, would I give you a stone?" whispered a voice in my heart. I voice I recognised and trusted. The voice that had been my companion since leaving the psychiatric unit almost twenty years before. A voice that was quieter than the dogmas and doctrines that had been holding my mind for so long. The voice that had eventually led me to leave it all behind. Sometimes it was hard to hear under the fear. But that day in the car driving up a misty Welsh hillside, there was no mistaking it.*

*It was that which gave me the courage to ask my question in the group later that morning after we had been exploring the symbolism of different animals. Even with the confidence that the quiet voice had given me, I had waited until the very end of a session, just as we were breaking for coffee. "Horrible creatures, they bring death, plucked the eyes out of some of our baby lambs," the owner of the farm answered forcibly.*

*I was stunned into silence. My heart was pounding in my ears as fear once again tore through my body making me tremble. Perhaps I hadn't heard that voice in the car, maybe these ravens visiting me were evil, maybe I was making a huge mistake.*

*But then a quiet voice brought me out of the tumult of my thoughts, very still and calm. She began to talk to be about ravens. How they are both predator and carrion feeder, clearing up the debris of death. How in many traditions they were thought to go between the worlds, that they were not afraid to go into the unseen realms where others feared to go, bringing wisdom out of darkness. As she talked, her voice very quiet and calm, I felt the fear seeping away. "Raven sounds like an ideal companion to have in your work," she said, reaching out and laying her hand on mine. "There is nothing to fear."*

*Raven reminds me not to look away. He says that the ancestors, including the other than human beings who once walked with us, can help us find ways through the challenges we face."*

**Polly Patton Brown**

# It is Time

It is time, it is time. But for what? I look askance at each mushroom, greet each bird as I walk in the woods, but they give me no clues. The bluebells stay silent, only the heron flies, knowing the way between yesterday and tomorrow.

I am mute. Fingers burrowing in leaf mulch looking for mycelial answers to the questions I dare not give breath to.

*Give me answers but not death,* I pray.

I have spent my life playing hide and seek with myself. I am tired of it.

I feel a part of me dying, the shell of my old self is peeling off. I fear there is nothing underneath.

*This is crazy. There's nothing wrong.*

The mantle of motherhood hangs heavy on my shoulders.

It initiated me into the body of my womanhood, the mystery of birth. It also curtails the self that needs to emerge now. It tethers me in the daily world, pulling my focus away from the strange shifts inside that I can feel.

I am drained from my work. Detached from myself.

I long to fly free.

To head into the dark woods alone

And to (finally, fully) embody who I have always sensed I am.

It is time to follow my inner voice… and the strange images that have been emerging, into the shadow places, into the unknown. The places that have always scared me.

To claim an identity that makes me shake.

To step into my weird wild self fully.

At last.

"I am talking here about a time when I began to doubt the premises of all the stories I had ever told myself, a common condition but one I found troubling... In what would probably be the middle of my life I wanted still to believe in the narrative and in the narrative's intelligibility, but to know that one could change the sense with every cut."

Joan Didion, *The White Album*

That was my plan. A strange one that I had committed to… despite not even understanding what it really meant. I tried to rationalise it. Make it into this or that. I tried to discuss it with a therapist. With friends. To draw it, write it, to find its shape and know its size.

All I knew was that it was time.

This scares me. I do not know how to be any different. I find myself drawn inwards to quietness, slowness, magic and mystery. I find myself pulled away from the house and out to the world of mushroom, crow and fallen leaf. And yet my life does not allow this. I must perform dutiful mother and busy working woman to the world, meanwhile a part of me is longing for the space to descend once more, to crouch in the leaf litter, to dive into my books of art and symbols and plants, to wonder and wander… I need to spend hours with words and images, shifting them back and forth, searching them like an oracle, for answers to a question I cannot fully articulate. And yet the washing up must be done, the train arrives at 4:40, the dinner will not cook itself.

I realise I have abandoned myself and been abandoned in turn.

The words have gone. The images too. I feel blank. Knowing what I can't say, mustn't do. I am scared and stuck. I am so tired of this. I go to pick up a pen, to step once again into that strange flow that the image of the caped figure emerged from. Nothing comes. A blank screen stares back at me. My inner critic stands in my way scoffing and scorning.

I pray to finally find my own artistic style, a voice which is mine. Instead of constantly doing battle with the inner critic each time I put pen to paper.

Instead, I find myself pulled. Flailing. Not being able to dedicate myself to work or family or soul.

The voices within echo the voices without. I have become crowded out of my own body, my own mind.

This is when the crow goddess calls, and the woods begin to shimmer, when the wild soul breaches.

I sense, somewhere deep within, that it is time.

I head out to the woods once more.

"You have to wonder if women are most free to let themselves go when they leave child-bearing behind them. I have only just discovered that the bones of women become aerated, filled with bubbles of air, and thinner, as they grow older, just like the hollow bones of birds. Sometimes this makes them frail. But perhaps, also, this lightness of limbs enables flight. It allows us to let go."

Julia Baird, *Phosphorescence*

# Shamanic Companion

*"On a retreat with the writer and teacher of shamanic ways, Manda Scott, the crow came large and as a companion within my journeying, dreaming and in waking. Wherever I went there was Crow. Even as I left that retreat in Wales and was given a lift home by a new-found friend, we were followed by crows the whole journey back, low flying, cawing and making their presence known. As we pulled up to my house crows sat upon the roof, to greet me.*

*I dreamt of Crow during that weekend away, taking me on its back flying at dusk, we flew over and near to a small child, her back to us, face in palms, quiet and still. She looked vulnerable and in need of care, the crow turned its head to me as we flew in circles above her "you don't wish to be heard?" We fly off as Crow's question lingers with me. As I wake, Crow speaks and repeats the question again.*

*That dream with Crow was in 2021 and only now, almost two years later, am I coming to see its message — that I was that child. All the dark shame and unspoken truths of my child self which still were hidden within began to find a voice, slowly and painfully over this period of time. 'We now wish to be heard' thanks to Crow."*

**Nicola Wood**

# A Fork in the Road

The light is dimming.
The sound of a gun. Then another.
The crows scatter.

Shadows lengthen.
A voice calls out, urgently.

*Stop!*
*Get back!*
You know this voice, perhaps better than your own.
This is the voice of the Shadow Master.
*Beware! Step away! Stay on the safe path!*

You have followed his orders most of your life.
You have minded the scarecrows,
Shirts stuffed with straw.
You have jumped and fled at the sound of the bird scarer,
The sharp shots of the gun seemingly aimed right at you.
You have heeded their warnings.
Obeyed their commands.
Avoided the barbed wire.
Stayed on the path.
Been good.

You have come to a fork in the road.
You try to choose between left and right –
Choices you have spent much of your life fretting about –
But they are inconsequential. Both are the same loop.

But look!
Look again.
Look closer…
There is another way. Less clear. But there, nonetheless.
A way in to the heart of the woods
Through the shadows.
Led by the crow.
Do you dare this time?

# Into the Unknown

I am searching. But for what I do not know. The path? The answer? Myself?
Everything is unclear. All I know is that something big is shifting: inside, outside.
The way things were could no longer hold.

The path I was walking was no longer mine.

You cannot both simultaneously know and not know, be and not be. Die and live.

And yet here it is. Here we are. Here I am.

What form to take? Where to start? Where to aim for? Destination unknown, anywhere but here.

It scares me. It doesn't make sense. And yet still the unknown calls me insistently.

In the voice of a crow.

"I worry what I'm risking if I follow
you into the unknown."

Aurora, "Into the Unknown"

# A Disappearing Act

I pause for a long time in this place. Indecisive. Unsure of what is the greater danger. Uncertain of what lies ahead – revelation, death, madness or perhaps even worse: nothing.

I feel myself becoming more and more ghostlike to the outside world, attempting the trick of disappearing myself in plain sight. It is a strange spell.

I am not wanting to die – at least not most of the time – simply to unbecome the self I have been, and become who I have always been... in the shadows. I have spent a lifetime trying to hide for safety, to make myself up, cutting myself into tiny pieces to fit into the shape of others' expectations. To hide what? From whom? I don't know. All I know is that being who I want to be, who I actually am, feels like it will cost my life. And so, I hide it away.

I am tired of trading my truth for other people's, of assimilating and accommodating. But this is what we were taught – the original sin of our own inherent wrongness. We learn to fear ourselves, override our instincts, see through the eyes of others first and last. We learn to discount our own seeing, to question our own knowing. For fear of what if...

I need to disappear.

But disappearing becomes harder when you have distilled yourself into a million words and slipped between the covers of a hundred thousand books and allowed yourself to be posted out in slivers of dead tree around the world. When you have created a family and business where people need you.

I want to peel off people like dead skin. I long for an invisibility cape so that they cannot see me.

I feel drawn to the woods. I have a feeling the trees hold the answers. Perhaps they can call me back to myself. Or rather call up a new self. I do not know. All I know is there are shadows everywhere.

In me.

Outside.

In order to know what will be, I have to forget all I have known before. And this too? The leaves fall as if in reply.

# Shadow

The dark wood is a place of shadows. In Jungian psychology – the ideological framework that makes most sense to my internal experiences – the shadow is where we put all the parts of ourselves that do not align with our desired identities. Some Jungians assert that alongside each of our personal shadows, there is a collective shadow of all the denied and repressed values of our culture.

The shadow – collective and personal – is a place that we cannot directly 'see' for ourselves, but often experience these qualities when we project them onto others.

We can witness this in our culture in the denial of the energies and qualities of the feminine and wild nature, which have been cast onto the symbols of the crow, the mushroom, the woods and the woman of power. These symbols have become holders of our culture's collective projected shadow, feared and rejected.

This projection of the shadow onto the Other, led to cultural dominance and prosperity, but is now coming to haunt Western culture. The crows, as the saying goes, are coming home to roost, as all the people who have been oppressed by patriarchy, all the damage that has been done to our ecosystems, is coming to light at the same time, leaving our cultures flailing from one crisis to the next, blind to their common root.

We inhabit a world of shadows, no longer aware of what casts them or why, we live in fear of their exaggerated forms, cowering within ourselves. We live in fear of the unseen, the unknown.

"To go in the dark with a light is to know the light.
To know the dark, go dark. Go without sight,
and find that the dark, too, blooms and sings,
and is traveled by dark feet and dark wings."

Wendell Berry,
*Terrapin: Poems by Wendell Berry*

# Crow Appears

Crow became an omnipresent image that I found myself working with day after day in my art. I tried in every medium I knew – acrylic, watercolour, fine liner pen, charcoal, oil pastel, pencil, eventually landing on pen and ink, a medium I had not used since my teens – trying to get past the impenetrable wall of my inner critic, to get past his ever-present voice, to meet Crow.

Each time I made an image, the critic's voice would chime up – *That's not... enough* – the realistic images were too safe, the freer images too childish. Nothing I did was good enough. I pushed and pushed and tried and tried. Until one day I decided to give my images the right of reply.

A messy crow emerged on the page – the inner critic swooped in once more. Instead of getting lost in internal wranglings I transcribed the voice of the critic there in black and white on the page until it had said what it needed to.

Then I allowed the crow to speak back:

*I am Crow...*

This was strange. Exciting. A different voice was emerging from this image: messy, brash, cheeky and very fucking clever.

The crow was... me, my inner creative self. The crow that had spent its life trying to be a dove, a sparrow, a peacock and failing. Because it was following the images and commands of others.

All along I was a crow.

The critic (who I came to call the Shadow Master – he who puppeteered my fears before my eyes) was my inner patriarch. The one who made the rules and hated crows. They were too noisy, too rude, too much, not enough... Over and over, he let me know his thoughts on me, my strange art and the crows.

I noticed a pattern: every time Crow showed up, the Shadow Master did too.

What did it all mean? I wasn't making it up or planning it. This reality that was unfurling on the paper in words and images before me had a life of its own, to which I was just a witness. I continued this process, allowing the paper to act as a sort of magic mirror, reflecting whatever hidden processes were going on below my conscious awareness, learning to trust the messy dark wisdom of Crow and to establish a different relationship with the Shadow Master.

This is the thing about seeking and following an image or a symbol. We are not making it up. It is guiding us to its central myth, hidden in the shadow of the psyche, it is leading us through the dark down to the rhizome, the root of the issue and ourselves, into the places we have always avoided.

The image, the journey, doesn't tend to make logical sense at the time. Often it is only in retrospect can you begin to put some sort of a shape on it. At the time it happens we are sourcing the information from the unconscious, guided by instinct: sometimes from the personal unconscious and sometimes deeper still from the collective unconscious, from that which we may previously have never been able to access with our waking mind. This is often threatening to our sense of who we present ourselves to be in the world. Threatening to the Shadow Master, as inner representative of the patriarchy.

Often during the creative process, information is coming through about something that is going on beneath the surface unseen, that we do not or cannot logically understand, a process of deep change: the transformation of the psyche.

"When an image calls to you, may you trust it."

Kim Krans, *The Wild Unknown Archetype Guidebook*

# Crow Speaks

"*The Crow Goddess came to me. I was not seeking, but she found me. I talk to animals; I always have. Normally, they don't talk back. But this time, I was out walking, spotted three crows at the roadside and said 'Hello' and, to my amazement, one of them answered, a perfectly audible 'Hello'!*

*As soon as I got home, I searched online. Was I mad? Was it even possible for wild birds to talk? And yes, it seemed, it was perfectly possible. Corvids are excellent imitators and can even repeat whole phrases.*

*The Crow is not like other birds. She is not delicate and sweet. She is intelligent, fierce, and free. Her voice is not soft, but rasping, loud. She laughs, she cackles, she screams. As I become older, as I transition from mother to middle age, I feel her presence more and more. She is not compliant. She does not fit in. She is not pretty, but has a wild, honest beauty. Most importantly, she has wings. And though she is feared, she is also respected. She is portal and paradox, a living contradiction – Three in One.*

*On my writing desk, I have three crow ornaments to inspire me. They guide me to other realms – places of fantasy only they and I know – and together we fly back, with words on our wings, ready to share with anyone else who has the ears to hear her.*"

**Rebecca Lowe**

# Metanoia

Carl Jung called this psychic process individuation: the conscious act of becoming fully one-self by working through the layers of the conscious and unconscious. In a healthy culture, individuation is a process that would happen as we leave home and establish ourselves in the adult world, supported by the community and rites of passage. Whereas in Western culture the lack of a rich psychologically supportive culture and meaningful rituals of initiation mean that this process is often aborted first time around and often happens instead at midlife.

The tides of midlife are strong, change is in the air: the unravelling of what has been; the tying off of fertility and child-raising; the loss of drive or idealism and the first flush of excitement. Death becomes a more frequent visitor in our lives. The body count of loved ones lost begins to mount and our own health may start to flounder. This is a time when our energy switches from pushing out into the world and proving ourselves to others, fulfilling their desires and expectations of us – training, building a reputation, birthing and raising our families – to having the resources available to revisit the process of psychological development. For women who menstruate this time has a biological marker as hormones shift, impacting our inner world, often in seismic ways.

As midlife settles into our bones, we may start to reassess our understanding of Self, and how it is expressed in the world. We may question previous priorities, boundaries, urges, the way we have worked and what we have allowed to limit us. In time we may find ourselves poised on the brink of becoming who we always felt we were meant to be, but in younger years were too scared, too busy, too distracted or immature to embody.

Tired and disillusioned, our bodies begin to ache and complain, we try to put on the mask of normal to reassure the world. Meanwhile we travel a dark inner path alone.

Midlife is a time when the Self of the first half of our lives often passes away and a void is created. What was once right and true is no more. A new horizon is drawing us in strangely, haltingly, roughly – an uncertain transition to an unknown land emerging on its own timing. We may find ourselves at a loss, waiting for another – hopefully a more authentic – version of Self to step into. It is strange and uncomfortable work.

*Do I fight it or surrender?* We find ourselves wondering. *Is it just my body that is changing, or my whole identity? Where am I going? How will it end? Who am I now?*

This experience is often referred to as metanoia, from the ancient Greek word meaning "changing one's mind."[13] Jung used the term to refer to "a spontaneous attempt of the psyche to heal itself of unbearable conflict by melting down and then being reborn in a more adaptive form – a form of self healing often associated with the mid-life crisis and psychotic breakdown, which can be viewed as a potentially productive process."[14] Metanoia represents a shift away from the well-established persona, towards the shadow and the larger Self, "a process which may be marked by a mixture of intensity, despair, self-surrender, and an encounter with the inner void."[15]

This was exactly what I had been experiencing.

"Typically, we encounter this dark forest at times of major life transitions. Although we may encounter the dark forest at any time in our life, there are some specific periods in life – times when we are about to leave a known way of being, and do not yet know how to be the next thing we are called to be – when we are most likely to enter the dark forest and be lost (for a time)."[16]

Dr Sushmita Mukherjee

# Initiated by Crow

"My relationship with Crow has been a complicated one. It began when the religion of my childhood became intolerable. I swapped organized religion for a nature-based, Celtic-inspired relationship. Cue Crow, as the untangling of conditioning began.

It was the summer I turned forty-nine that the crow first made its appearance in my life.

I was in my happy place where I felt most at home in my body. This is where crow began working with my spirit. It seemed everywhere I went that summer, crows would appear and make themselves known. They were in groups walking about my front yard, swooping overhead and landing in trees as I walked, following me the whole way. They became a constant companion wherever I went, no matter the locale. They even appeared in Ireland while I was exploring my roots there.

Interestingly, in the beginning, I had an antagonistic relationship with Crow energy. I felt as if they were taunting me and finding me lacking. I remember even shouting aloud in exasperation one morning, 'I am trying my best, goddammit!' After disclosing this to a wise friend, I received a re-frame from one of judgement to that of helper. She said, 'Crow is one of your spiritual helpers and shows itself when you need reassurance or need for safety.'

It was shortly after this teaching that I was gifted a dead, yet perfectly preserved crow in a frozen puddle on a walk in the forest. I had set an intention for feathers for a ceremonial saining stick before leaving, and found this beautiful offering mid-walk. It was with those tail feathers in hand, that I officially adopted Crow as my magickal helper and invited it into my spiritual journey.

My relationship with Crow has evolved since that day. Crows are a comforting presence and a reminder that I have allies in the sky who bring messages of support. I now chat with them and thank them for their company. Further insight has revealed that they are also fierce restorers of justice. These wise and powerful friends are a reminder that I am not alone and that magick exists. In a time of great personal transition and uncomfortable threshold dwelling, they were of great comfort. I will always celebrate the spirit of Crow in my life."

**Kelley Davis Sookram**

# Impenetrable

My feet take me through the woods once more. Off the main track and onto smaller paths I have been too scared to walk alone before. My mind races:

*What if people see me and think I'm crazy? What if I get lost and never find my way home? What if some crazy murderer or rapist is lying in wait in the shadows?*

My brain is tired. The branches of my nervous system are brittle. My energy sapped. Autumn is here inside, outside. My feet walk, head resists.

*Be careful, stay safe.*

But still my feet insist on walking.

My mind turns this experience over and over.

Getting nowhere.

I stand cold and alone. Longing for comfort and answers.

Moon and crow, tree and mushroom: there is something there. Something big and deep and wide and ancient below the surface. The connection, the relationship, the energetic or symbolic bond. My mind cannot scratch the itch. It cannot read what it is. Yet another part knows. Beyond words.

*How do I get there?*

OOO

Impenetrable.

This is what the forests are to the mind.

This is what the soul is to the brain.

We cannot see the trees for the wood.

Cannot see our deepest selves with our own eyes.

We live blind and bound

To the visions and stories of others.

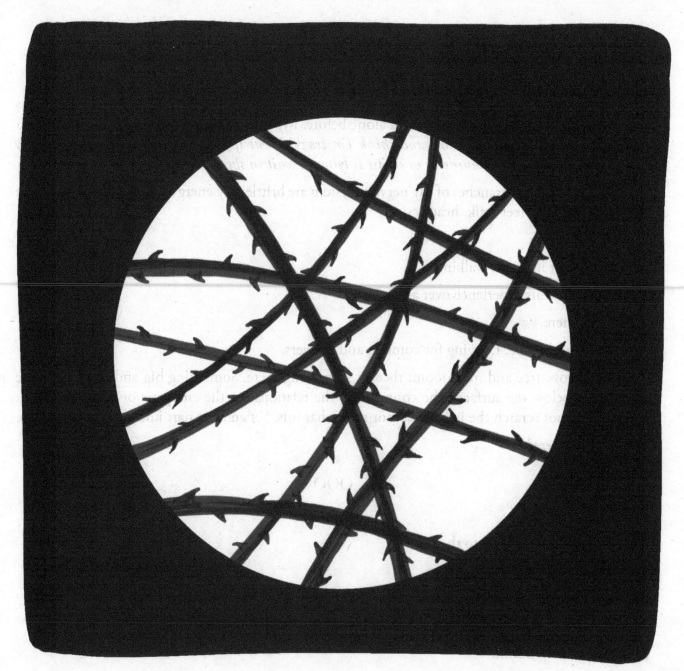

Briars. Thick and thorny, weave between tree trunks, a wall of spikes as tall as a man, barring our way into the heart of the woods.

When you walk into the wild wood, into the wood within, you will encounter this living wall of thorns that snare the unwary passer-by who tries to breach their barricade. They have millions of years of evolution of doing just this.

The briars are not your friend. You will not get past without a plan and some tools: a goat, some secateurs, a machete, digger, hedgecutter, flail, magic wand… or at the very least a sturdy stick and a heart full of courage.

On this journey into the dark woods that I have worked on many levels – real world, image, energetic, linguistic and psychic – it is the briars that get you every time. They are your most worthy opponents, admirable adversaries. All it takes it a snippet of stalk, a sliver of root and up they spring once more.

At one foolhardy point I found myself entirely wrapped in real-life brambles. Around my legs, catching my hem, around my scarf, my throat, my hair, my hands. They seemed to have will, intention. Like the man-eating plants of science fiction. I was completely and utterly snared. Prey to a plant.

Panic was my go-to response, but that was not going to help release me from their grasp. No one knew I was here. The more I struggled, the more ensnared I became.

And so, I stopped and took a deep breath and began, one by one, to unpick the thorns that held me.

This is the work we do on the inner forest too. Unpicking the fear briars that are caught in our minds, holding us hostage. Struggling against them simply makes them dig in stronger.

This was another lesson of the forest. A painful one. But it wasn't finished yet. Because truth is always far stranger than fiction if we allow ourselves to stop and see where the inner and outer realms overlap.

There, where I'd been snared – just by my feet – was a bloom of late-season mushrooms. The biggest I had ever seen in this wood. Almost as though the briars were wanting to stop me in my tracks. To make me look closer.

This 'gift' came at a price. I was picking thorns out of my hands for a week. The journey to the heart of the forest demands sacrifice. It will give you insight, mushrooms, berries, Crow Moons and memories. But always in exchange for a scratch, a scrape. A muddy bottom. Dog shit on the shoe. A twisted ankle. A broken bone. Or in my case a tuft of hair, several of drops of blood, two hands full of thorns and a snag in my favourite scarf, the thread unravelling…

# Unravelling

I am slowly unravelling. I have lost the thread of myself. I feel like I am falling apart on the inside, falling further and further out of synch with the world, with understanding anything. I feel like a woman on the verge, on the edge, on the brink, poised over the precipice I have backed away from many times fearing madness or death.

I'm in almost constant pain. I've had enough. Time is slipping away from me.

This is a wordless place. And yet I insist on trying to put words to it. To be able to roll it around my mouth, to share it with others.

The thread spools.

Fabric comes apart in my hands.

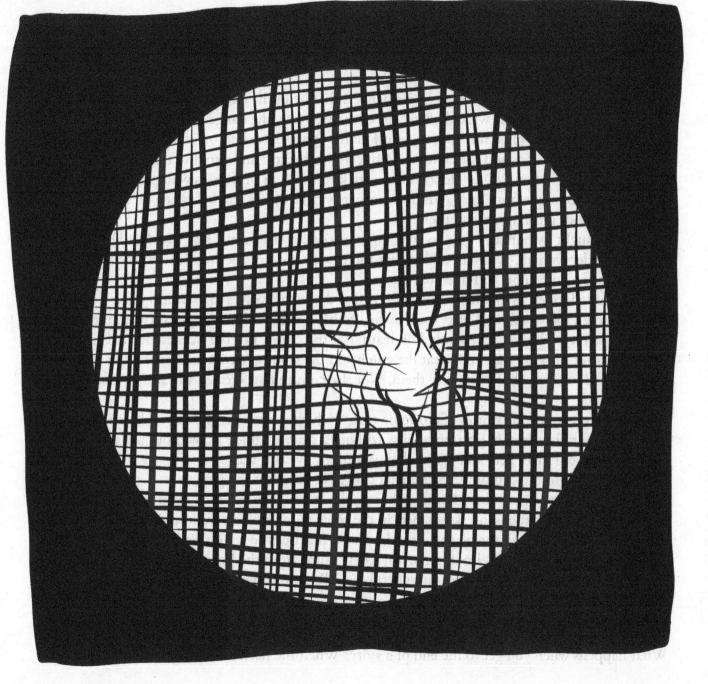

# Losing the Plot

In our childhood we were warned of the dangers that lie in the dark woods: the poisonous mushroom, the wild wolf, the wicked witch, the enchanted tree, the danger of losing our way. We were taught to be good girls, not to wander off alone. We were reared on stories of the gingerbread house deep in the woods and the children who scattered breadcrumbs to find their way safely home. Or the tale of naïve Red Riding Hood and the trickster wolf, of princesses who pricked their fingers or ate a poisoned apple from the hands of a cunning wicked queen and fell asleep for a hundred years whilst the woods grew up around them.

We were taught by our fairy tales to curb our appetites, scorn magic, fear woodland creatures and revile the older woman. We were told to fear the woods and not the woodcutter, the wolf and not the hunter, the raven not the Ravenmaster.

They omitted to tell us that it was the hunters that drove the wolves to extinction, the woodcutters who cut down the woods and used them as fuel to burn the witches, the priests who hurt the children. It was men who were the symbol of death, not the crows, not the women decried as witches.

In story after story we learned to fear the witch and the woods. We learned to fear the magical. To fear the shadows, not those that cast them. Not the culture that created the stories and wrote the history books.

We no longer know the stories of old to be true: we have grown beyond fairy tales and gods. And so, we find ourselves here in postmodernity, without a story to guide us, without a myth to call our own. We find ourselves here and realise that we cannot live this way.

We have come to the end of the patriarchal story. We have lost the plot.

In the place of the gingerbread cottage is a bank, in place of the rookery an airport, instead of mushrooms a mall, a thousand skyscrapers in the place of ten million trees, and the clogged arteries of roads winding through the place where the sacred heart of the woods used to be.

The scattered breadcrumbs leading the way safely home from the heart of the forest were eaten by the crows long ago. Now they feast on our rubbish. Ravenous beaks in fried chicken tubs, picking the bones clean.

Watching us. Waiting.

What happens when you get to the end of a story? When the narrative frays, the thread unspools?

This is where I am. Where we are. Disenchanted with the world, with our culture, our lives, our selves. Running out of meaning.

The world as we know it is dying and we don't know what to do.

We are disconnected from ourselves, from each other, from the natural world.

Our frenzied culture cannot admit that the story is ending.

Yet we are still alive.

Just.

Picking at the bones

Wondering: *what happens next?*

"Modern man does not understand how much his 'rationalism' (which has destroyed his capacity to respond to numinous symbols and ideas) has put him at the mercy of the psychic 'underworld.' He has freed himself from 'superstition' (or so he believes), but in the process he has lost his spiritual values to a positively dangerous degree. His moral and spiritual tradition has disintegrated, and he is now paying the price for this break-up in world-wide disorientation and dissociation."

C.G. Jung, *Man and his Symbols*

"The man who thinks he can live without myth, or outside it, is an exception. He is like one uprooted, having no true link either with the past, or with the ancestral life which continues within him, or yet with contemporary human society. [...] The psyche is not of today: its ancestry goes back many millions of years. Individual consciousness is only the flower and the fruit of a season, sprung from the perennial rhizome beneath the earth; and it would find itself in better accord with the truth if it took the existence of the rhizome into its calculations. For the root matter is the mother of all things."

C.G. Jung, preface to the 4th English edition of *Symbols of Transformation*

# The End

The End.

That is how the stories of childhood ended.

Usually, they all lived happily ever after.

But in older, darker fairy tales, there was a loss. A permanent change of the status quo. A moral. And then the story ended.

This is the end. But of what I am not sure. I am haunted by the loss, with no clue of what precisely I will be mourning. I only know that things must change, are changing, inside, outside.

This cycle is done.

But I don't know what comes next. Only that it scares me. And I am tired.

Experiencing a major life transition in a world in transition is distinctly unsettling. Usually when our inner worlds are shaken like snow globes, we look outside ourselves and are able to experience a sense of being held by the cycle of the seasons going on around us, as they always have. The reassuring rhythms of the ecological world beyond reminding us of our place in the scheme of all things, gently lulling us back into rhythm, co-regulating us back into synch with reality.

But the rhythms of nature are breaking down. Because of us. This year the mushrooms are a month late, because there has been no rain. Violets and rhododendrons, usually seen in April are blooming in mid November. We mark the warmest Armistice Day on record. And in the midst of it all, truth has flown away, no one can agree on anything, everyone believes at least a third of humanity is insane and dangerous. We are at each other's throats, fighting over previously held certainties that we can neither prove nor disprove entirely.

On my walks I watch, helpless, as they cut swathes through the wood, harvesting trees. Piles of logs stacked high along the path waiting to be transported out into the world on massive lorries. They see resources ready to be harvested. I see piles of bodies.

We should be planting trees not clearing them.

The logging tracks are slick with mud, hampering their removal. The rains fall. I am grateful for small mercies.

I resist the cocoon which calls my name. We have already had too many winters.

I long for mellow days of mushrooms, but already the rooks are roosting in the trees, dark thought birds settle in my mind. The days are so short they could snap in two like a wishbone between your fingers. But this time you don't know if the wish is one you dare to take or if it is a devil's pact of darkness.

It is getting weirder in the twilight; the crows are circling once more. It is time.

But for what?

I wait.

And wait.

Cold settling into my bones.

Coat threadbare.

Still, I wait.

The second winter darker still, colder, but no clearer.

More trees cut.

Meanwhile my body and mind contort and refuse to do the thing called daily life. Meanwhile the outer moon begins to lose its pull on my inner tides and takes up residence in my right eye.

Meanwhile I flounder.

Meanwhile the world dives into ever-more-scary death spirals.

Death is everywhere. But everyone is too busy to care.

Too clever to believe it. Too scared to run. Too bored to bother.

Too numb to feel the impending ending.

Too blind to see the new beginnings.

And here in the world as it always was, everything is disintegrating, and nobody cares.

The trees wave their warning. The rains flood and withhold.

Forests burn, cliffs liquify, rivers break their banks.

Earth cracks open. Buildings fall.

Again and again and again.

Outside, above, below is falling apart.

The crows on the rooftops caw from their vantage point.

We draw the curtains, turn up the volume. Eyes on screens, doomscrolling, watching, watching, waiting for it to finally happen. Whatever it is. To know what the ending is going to be in order to know who we should be and what we should do.

# Wake Up!

*"Where I live in Maine, I hear many crows calling throughout the day. I've always liked them, and a few years ago I opened myself to a deeper relationship. Now their caws have become my 'mindfulness bell.' They come when I don't anticipate them, break into my awareness, and remind me 'Wake up! Are you here, right here, or are you lost somewhere else in your mind?'*

*As best as I can remember to do it, I stop, breathe, and come into the present. To honor this crow medicine, I created a little figure named Hineni, a Hebrew word frequently said by characters in the Old Testament when called on by the Holy. I am here, I am willing. Thank you, crows, for reminding me."*

**Cindy Read**

# Crow Calls

Look up!
She's perched on the roof of your home, calling, calling. Her voice is blackness.
Calling you out, calling you in.

Calling you.

You have tried to dispel the knowing that she is calling you. Ignored the goddess on the wing trying to tell you something.

Crow: guardian of the Otherworld.

Bird of darkness. Initiator.

Bringing messages of change and death.

The heart of the dark woods is calling

In the voice of a crow

Right outside your window.

Do you hear?

Will you follow her now?

"I have a strong sensation that the crows are carrying messages for me, but that perhaps I'm not quite listening well enough, or that I'm somehow overlooking the point. I'm not sure what to do with the sensation that I'm supposed to be learning or doing something specific, like something is palpably waiting for me to figure it out, to discover it. I can sense a next step close by."

Molly Remer, *Walking with Persephone*

# Holding Back

What keeps us from heeding the voice of the crow? From following her, heading out from the town. Out beyond. Beyond safety and reason, beyond answers and understanding, beyond existing narratives. Into the shadow spaces. Into the unknown. Into the selves that are waiting for us.

Fear.

White bone fear.

Black night terror.

Wild beast.

Man beast.

The fear that darkness equals death.

Darkness leads to madness.

Fear of being a woman alone in the shadows.

Of meeting the one who casts shadows.

Maybe even of realising that we

Are the ones that cast shadows

Haunting ourselves.

The fear, the fear, the fear…

Death, death, death…

The fear lies in dark places.

When transformation calls our name.

When grief and loss and dissolution appear.

To devour us.

To destroy us.
To unravel us.
To transform us.
What do we do
When the story ends
But death is not yet here?

# Harbingers of Initiation

In many cultures the crow is known as a psychopomp – a character or creature that guides the dead to the afterlife, one who moves between two worlds. In Jungian psychology the psychopomp – sometimes a wise person, and sometimes an animal ally – assists us in moving between the realms of the conscious and unconscious.

Crow is one of its common forms.

I discover that "crow and raven are symbols of nigredo, the first stage of alchemy and represent dying to the world."[17]

There are no coincidences here.

Each initiation of the soul tends to have a symbol that emerges to lead us through the disintegration of our old reality: a word, a guiding image, a new name…

For me it was the crow, the figure in the long black cape and the Crow Moon.

"Crows are harbingers of initiation. [They] bring wisdom and warning [...] signal periods of rupture."

Amanda Yates Garcia, *Initiated*

# Crow as Initiator to Death

*"One afternoon I was sat working in my home office… I heard a scratching on the roof above, bird claws scraping frantically against the slate tiles. It grew louder and louder still. It was quite unnerving; my heart was pounding hard in my chest. Then suddenly like a cascade of black water pouring off the roof at least twelve crows fell to the grass right under my window, swirling, flapping, squawking and screeching intensely. I couldn't tell where one crow ended and another began, it was one huge furious cloud of flapping blackness.*

*It felt like they were screaming at me, shaking me awake to a piercing presence, opening me to receive and perceive their message and medicine.*

*'A doorway is opening near you soon, get ready, you are a soul midwife, a guardian, a death doula. Engage consciously so you can stay rooted, your energy will be called forth, watch your dreams, ready yourself.'*

*Two days later my best friend's mum passed away. Two weeks after that another friend's mother passed away in very difficult circumstances.*

*I held space for my friends, attending funerals, sitting with their pain. I walked the souls of both mothers across the veil and have done many times since. Crow is my totem of the ultimate transformation from matter back into Spirit. Back home."*

**Kimberley Jones**

# Threshold

To the awakening one, life holds many thresholds, many portals of initiation.

Of which death is the final one.

You are at such a threshold.

The place where you cannot see forward, and you cannot go back.

A place of dark possibility.

Take a breath.

Leave an offering.

Ask for a blessing.

Look for a door, a sign.

Keep listening.

Keep your eyes open, your mind soft.

"In psychotherapy, a woman must submit to the discipline of introversion and muster the courage to face her demons. Otherwise no transformation is possible. [...] Crossing the threshold [...] requires facing the abyss of the unknown. A woman fears and resists taking the first step. While consciously she only wants to solve the current problem, she nonetheless intuits that her deeper self may pull her into a process she never envisioned. Analysis will challenge her to unequivocally see herself and others and make it incumbent on her to act on what she learns. Once she has embarked on that path, there is no going back. Often, when confronted with a particularly difficult truth by her unconscious, a woman will ruefully say, 'I wish I could go back to being blissfully ignorant.' But she is fully aware that she cannot turn away from the knowledge she now possesses; she must go forward and face the next threshold."

Virginia Beane Rutter in *Crow Mother and the Dog God*

# Initiation

Each initiation gives us another opportunity to be recreated anew, but it requires sacrifice too, leaving behind what we have loved and known ourselves to be.

To slip into the magic we must shift our seeing, soften our thinking, slow down our minds. We must become entrained by a silent rhythm.

We must notice the details, learn them by heart.

Inside, outside.

We slow down.

And then some more.

Listening, listening.

Watching, waiting.

Noticing.

Slowing our racing minds

Down to the pace of the woods.

Until we ourselves come more clearly into focus, becoming familiar, another creature of the woods.

Until we are held in a mutual gaze

Of kinship

Shared belonging to this strange and wonderful world

That is momentarily painted anew.

These moments – what I call Crow Moons – are ephemeral, often with no proof for their having happened except for the fact that they have transformed the witness. They are moments when we experience the transcendent. When, for a moment, we and the whole of reality are one. Our inner world merges with the outer world and we experience a state of flow. This shift in vision, in consciousness, this momentary gnosis, often leads to a revelation that changes everything. An insight that goes on to shape an individual's life or create a movement.

"Keep an open mind to all things... Banish fear. Embrace your courage. Use your eyes. Perhaps you use your physical eyes too much and only see the mask. Find your eyes within. Look for the door into the unknown country."

Pixie Colman Smith

It may begin with a fizz or a jolt, it might feel like a furring and fuzzing, a flitting or a buzzing. A shift. Where reality as you know it goes out of focus for a moment and something ancient and shimmering takes its place. The world becomes simultaneously more fluid and more solid at the same time.

It can happen anywhere. But the woods are perhaps the best place to start. Somewhere away from the bustle of everyday life, where we can sink into the mud of our being unseen. Where we can drop the rules of the modern world and become our ancient selves.

With a flip and a fuzzing, the woods move from a place of trees and briars, stones and mud, to something else, something more. You have stepped through a portal into another realm.

This doesn't happen by floating over but by seeing through. By immersing ourselves in the details.

All is entangled.

Reality is morphing and strange.

Hear that rustle? Over there. In the dark.

Follow it. Keep going.

Do you see?

The moving shadow just out of your vision.

Follow it. Listen close. Do not get distracted by fear or your phone. The crows are calling you. The moon is rising.

Allow yourself to grow smaller. Small as an earwig. To crawl between the roots.

Allow yourself to grow feathers, wings.

Here you can soar and nest in the tallest trees.

Burrow into the cool earth.

See with your feet. Hear with your fingertips. Touch with your eyes. Smell with your forked tongue. Know with your guts.

Here you are.

You.

Wild and weird.

This is the place of witches and wild creatures. The realm of mycelium and mother tree. Fox and weasel. The birds are watching. There are eyes everywhere.

Here the clock has no power, the rules do not apply.

Here the seasons still hold sway, sun and moon, rain and snow.

The rolling headlines of impending doom cannot touch you here.

Instead, the news comes on the wing of crow and song of thrush, the blooming of blackthorn and falling of maple, the rush of river and squelch of mud.

They are what is real, what matters most.

Listen to what they have to say.

Let your losses fall from your arms

And look.

What for?

# Sign

A feather, a feather!
Pick it up, and look.
What do you see?
The white shaft, the black barb-like hairs.
An iridescent sheen that speaks of magic.
Look deeper still.
What do you see?
A gift? A magic wand?
An amulet? An omen?
A message? A quill to write your own story?
An invitation? A key?

# The Key

The key, the key!
I have found the key… but where does it fit?
Where is the door to which it belongs?
Is it behind me or in front?
Is the moon a door?
I pray for answers…
It does not bode well.
I rattle everything I pass that might be a door.
Still the night rises.
Dark and strange.
It is time, it is time.
But for what?
Still, I don't know.
Still, I resist.

"Getting through the door is never really the hard part, although we may think so at the time. Though we may have expended a lot of effort to get to the entrance itself, to find the key and go through the door, the real difficulty in engaging with the self lies on the other side, waiting in the darkness. All disciplines have crucial testing thresholds, thresholds that ask us if we are serious or ask us if we want to turn back and do something else. If we are equal to the test, it is also a time when we realize the greater import of what we have dedicated ourselves to. At this threshold we find that there are dimensions that have absolutely nothing to do with our particular comfort or happiness, that in actual fact we are involved with others as much if not more than ourselves and that this takes an ability to actually get beyond that small self that first searched for the key and turned it in the door."

David Whyte, *The Three Marriages*

# Portal

The beginning of initiation is darkness.
The beginning of initiation is an unsettling
Of the world, of your perception, of who you are and what you know.
An unsettling of reality.
Crows, by their nature, are unsettling.
That is their role.
Always, always.

Wildness calls your soul
In the voice of the crow
A billion black feathers flurry.
Darkness falls.
Allow yourself to sink into it.
The moon is rising.
Crow Moon.

The portal is opening.
A liminal space between the worlds.
Here you stand at the entrance
En-tranced.

Your portal place does not need to contain birds nor a moon,
(Though often they do.)

But what they do require is a human, waiting, willing,

Open to a shift in perception.

Willing to step through the veils of this reality

And into themselves and the world more fully.

This is the moment you have been waiting for.

Looking, but not finding.

Until suddenly it appears, when you least expect it.

In a form that surprises you.

And you will know, at last…

It is time

To step through.

# Full Moon

The full moon rises.
  I find myself not in a forest, but a darkened room. I find myself bed-bound with migraines for weeks on end. The outside world is too bright and loud. Endless nausea haunts me.

Images emerge from the darkness.

My eye a glowing full moon.

Surreal visions emerging from the morphing light and patterns that hijack my right eyeball, which becomes a strange moon. Shining day and night.

Reality swirls like autumn leaves.

Crows.

The hooded figure.

The twilight.

Rising moon.

Black sky.

Mushrooms.

Branches, branches.

Real.

And unreal both.

Which is branch, which root? Which is underworld, which outer?

Is this real? Does this matter?

Wingers, fingers, flaws, claws, white blackness branching. Words like crows fly from my mouth. Chaotic. And still nothing. Nowhere. Here.

Am I disappearing or re-emerging?

Is it too late? For what?

I close my eyes and see branches. Black against the light of my eyeball.

I begin to draw again. Black square, white moon.

I start with branches. And more branches. Roots and mycelium. Branching.

I see the connection between the moon in my images and the bright shining moon in my eye.

Between the bare branches of the world outside and the black branching blood vessels within.

I notice that my almost endless migraines have become connected to my creative output. Each is preceded by a rush of images and proceeded by a rush of words.

Strange images.

Strong images.

"The moon represents the dark side of Nature, her unseen aspect; the spiritual aspect of light in darkness; inner knowledge; the irrational, intuitional and subjective."

J.C. Cooper,
*An Illustrated Encyclopedia of Traditional Symbols*

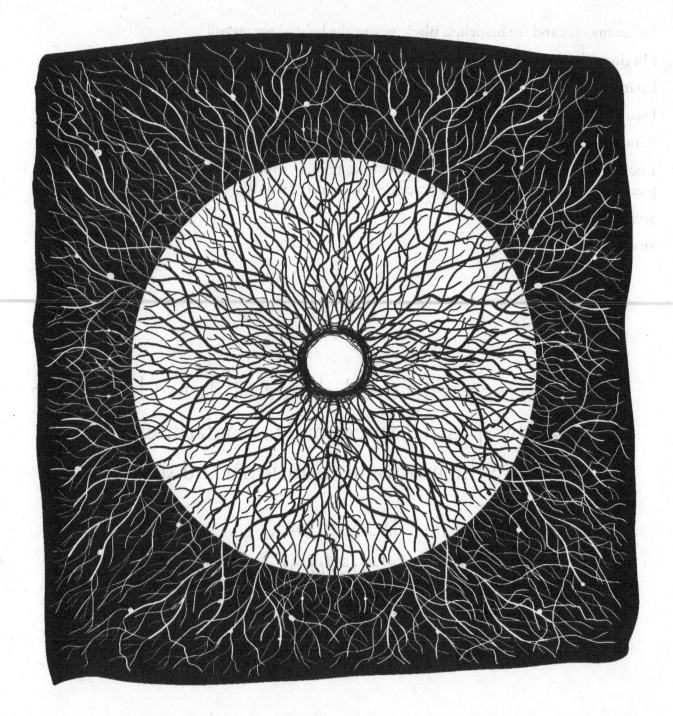

I am remembering a fluidity of self and soul as I move between the outer world of the woods and the inner images and words. I am in pain. Endless pain.

My bodymind is immersed in a different landscape, descending possessed by the shadows of other worlds, dreams, vivid shadowy images so close I can touch them.

The trick, I have found, is not to try to reproduce anything on the tip of my mind but instead allow them to reveal themselves through the light and shadow on the page, to allow my sight to shift so that the visions can emerge.

I can taste the truth of my soul again. I touch the place I have longed for in myself. And at the same time I cannot live my daily life which I long for.

I did not intend to trade one for another.

The images and words, inner and outer realities morph, new meaning is made. I make space for this inner strangeness to emerge, watching in awe as the weird flows from my fingers in black and white. In image after image, I try to capture what I had found in the woods. Not the literal forms of mushroom or crow, but surreal morphing images of trees and crows and moons and roots and mycelia. A dance of symbols. A swirling of form and energy. Images from the woods I walked mingle with images that emerge from the dark woods within, something just out of reach is shifting inside me, just as it did that evening when I first saw the Crow Moon.

One form morphs into the next. A curve becomes hair becomes a face, both ways up at the same time. A flame is a vulva is an eye is a never-ending possibility. This process opens up the world. Eyes are everywhere. One meaning shapeshifts into the next without the need for logical sense or representational accuracy. Instead, I am able to follow the energetic thread.

I immerse myself in the images. Migraine merging with the mundane world, where phantom smells and flickering vision come to me. All is heightened. Real, unreal and surreal become one.

No words but a black pool of wisdom: dark water emerging, flowing like a river, calling me. This is what I long more deeply for: connection to expression of this nameless place.

This is the place I have been missing, the place I was too scared to visit. The place that scares me with its strangeness.

This was not the path I intended to take. This was not the journey I had planned.

And yet, here I am.

Me and the moon – giver of night vision, puller of the tides, goddess on high – making magic together.

"There's a wildness within us that yearns to be physical, sensual, animal, free. But fear of this unknown part, of where it might take us and who it might make us, has left us all only half alive.

We live in a human world of comfort and possessions, safe and secure but cut off from the natural world, from our body, from the magic of embodiment. It's the Moon that illuminates our ancient longing. When it appears in the night sky of our soul, it's a holy grail finally within reach."

Phyllis Curott,
*The Witches Wisdom Tarot Guidebook*

# Dying to the World

Each initiation requires a death.

I am dying to the world, no wonder the crows called to me.

One of my physicians – a migraine sufferer herself – says that each migraine is like a mini death. This brings tears of recognition to my eyes. It is exactly how I feel. The truth of being felled by pain and light and sound, plans pushed aside, having to retreat into darkness for three days at a time, before gradually coming back to life.

It is sapping my will this faster and faster cycle of death and rebirth. My house is dark, curtains pulled tight against the light. It feels like there is almost nothing left of me. I don't know what the lesson is supposed to be. I feel like I am not learning it... except that the crow speaks of death, the caped figure speaks of death...

I have lost many dear ones in the past year. January is the darkest and most painful month yet. It feels like death is everywhere, darkness is everywhere, the cold and dark. The side effects of the drug that I am given for my migraines is suicidal ideation. For day after day after increasing my dosage death dances before my eyes, beckoning me.

"To yield to this dark place, to its unspeakableness, to give ourselves up to it we may recapture an essential organic rhythm of primordial layers of our unconscious processes."

Ann and Barry Ulanov, *The Witch and the Clown*

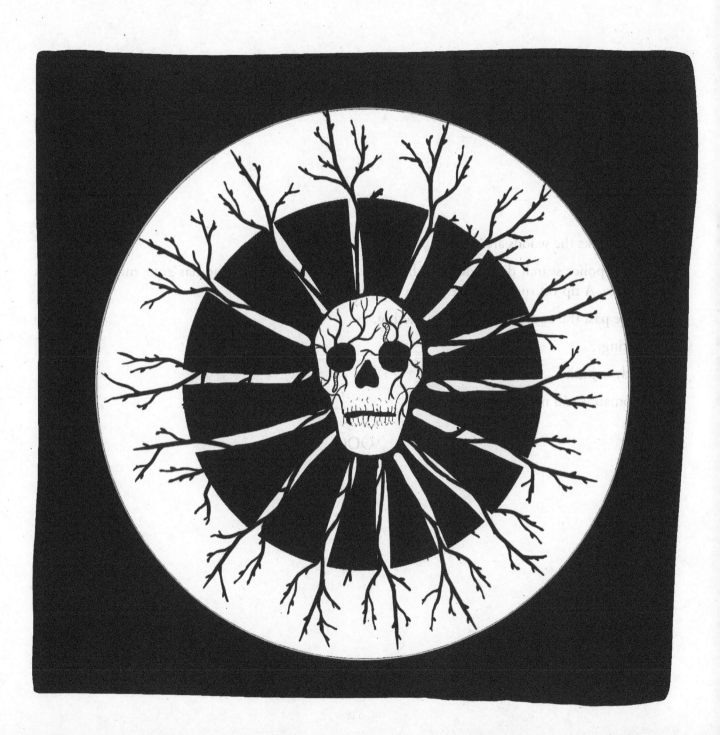

OOO

For weeks the woods are closed.

The police search the undergrowth for the body of a woman who has gone missing without trace. A tip-off suggested she was in this woodland.

We drive past the cordon each day wondering,

wondering…

No body is found.

The woman is still missing.

OOO

Here she lies.

Body curled under a blanket of leaves.

Here in the darkest reach of the forest.

The place where they bury the bodies.

She has been found.

Circled by crows.

Here lies the good girl who was afraid of being lost in the woods.

Here lies the good girl who followed the hooded one.

Here lies the good girl.

The forboding was right.

A death.

A death.

I prayed it would not be my loved ones.

My prayer was answered.

It was me.

# Between the Worlds

I find myself between the worlds.

Body breaking down.

Mind too.

I am composting.

Soul seeping out into the world.

Bleak nothingness.

Everything is meaningless.

Strange.

Unsettling.

This is the place of earthworm and earwig, leaf mould and mycelium.

A timeless realm of darkness.

# The Cloaked Figure

From the darkest darkness
A cloaked figure appears.
Black and hooded.

Back to me, I cannot see its face.

It pauses, as though waiting for me.

I feel its fate and mine are intertwined.

Though how I cannot say.

It is time.

This figure has haunted me for years, appearing again and again in my artwork. In films and dreams. In the swinging pendulum of the priestess divining my future in a basement temple in Crete.

Attracted and repelled.

My mind tries to get closer, to see it, to reason with it.

It evades me. Unsettles me.

I have always assumed it was Death.

And it is. Of a sort.

But it is not The End.

Under the surface, in the midst of the dying, life is stirring, pulsing, recycling, regenerating, reimagining… Psychic energy that has been stored underground erupts. Soul force emerges.

I draw the figure to me with words, images, rhythms and embodiment. Consciously reconnecting the disconnection, overriding the fear, allowing this energy through.

Her hooded head, her cloak…

The cloak can be a symbol of disguise, protection and initiation. It can hide one's true form or be the garb of ceremonial action. Which is hers?

I put pen to paper, another image appears.

The black cape, the path, the trees…

I look down and notice the tracks behind her – crow's feet – leading into the heart of the woods.

Crow's feet – the footprints of crow.

Crow's feet – the symbol of aging.

Crow's feet – the symbol of the witch and the wise woman.

A black feather falls from the cloak.

I follow.

# Meeting Bird Woman

Slowly,

Slowly she begins to turn.

And I stare in disbelief. It is her! Bird Woman! She has returned! I thought I might never see her again.

We have herstory, she and I.

Bird Woman first re-emerged in the transition time between projects, just as my writing of *She of the Sea* was coming to an end and *Crow Moon* was starting to emerge. I wrote there:

"I come from a long line of Bird Women.

I realise, as the image comes through me once again, that the struggle of the Bird Woman is that her soul longs to be free, but her body must remain grounded. The urge to jump [from the cliffs in the form of a bird] is not to crash and die, but to soar and fly."

It was then that I began to realise that Bird Woman was symbol of me, of my soul, but she was also something else, something ancient.

It was in my art-making that I first met her. In a picture I drew when I turned sixteen. The year my migraines started. There are no coincidences here.

There she was. There were most of the symbols that have haunted my art ever since.

There was the dreamer – myself – lying down, eyes closed.

And there was the key in the beak of the bird. Flying away.

There, in the corner of the image, is the shadowy figure. The dark caped one. Faceless. Ominous. Unknown but present.

This was the first image that I felt was truly of me. It was a strange combination of surrealism and symbolism, unlike anything that the other girls in my class were making. It held dark meaning for me. Truths I could not yet understand with my rational mind.

A few months later a Bird Woman appeared in another form. In a poster for the Stravinsky ballet *Firebird* – a woman with a cracked egg for a head leaping through flames. (Synchronistically *Firebird* was the name of the film that my brother was launching at the same time that I was writing *Crow Moon*.) Another image, "The Tragedy of Woman", depicted a masked woman, a magnifying

glass showing her real feeling in her eyes – the double-edged sword of fertility, a single tear in the form of a egg white and yolk, trickled down her cheek.

The Bird Woman images continued with sketches of me dressed in a feather boa, morphing into me growing wings, a beak and claws, standing on the edge of the cliffs, "Waiting to Fly". Whether this was going to be a death leap or a leap into faith, I did not know.

The final picture in the unintended series, was the bridges of Amsterdam rendered in black and white, spiralling down a plug hole.

After that I stopped following my inner stream of images for years, scared by my own strangeness. By the dark symbols that emerged. By the way that events would be clear to me before they happened – dreams and strange visions that would become realities: a death, a plane crash, figures appearing at the foot of my bed in the middle of the night, watching, waiting.

I was haunted by what was happening, what it meant. By whether it was real or not. By how mad it made me. After that I left Bird Woman alone. I consciously turned the tap of these images off, stepped away from my creativity. All I wanted was to fit in, to be normal. Not weird.

My mind, the way it worked, wasn't something that anyone understood. My experiences didn't seem to have much overlap with others around me. I tried medications for the migraines, for depression. Instead of healing and relief, they brought the images further to life, erupting in terrifying reality into my waking life with crows flying out of my eyes and demons talking to me. There were no cures for who I was, it seemed. And so, I pledged myself to the outside world, to work hard and achieve. To be good. I kept away from the strange inner self and the dark woods within and the Bird Woman who haunted them.

Looking back, I realise that my migraines emerged when the images did. They flared badly during the several months that I shut down my abilities. And then flared again in my forties when I decided to fully unleash them once more. There is no coincidence.

I also realise that these images poured from me a couple of years after my first bleeding. And that they emerge again a couple of years before my last blood. I recall that in my book *Moon Time*, I shared a quote from an unattributed Native American source that has resonated with so many women: "At her first bleeding a woman meets her power. During her bleeding years she practices it. At menopause she becomes it." This I was living as my truth. Even when I didn't even know what my truth was. It was living through me.

# The Gift

The wisdom that each of us gains during the initiation of the dark woods is different. For me, it is crow and the moon and the encounter with Bird Woman. For you, it might be something different. But for all of us, it is the gift of a long-lost expression of ourselves, a Self that we dare not claim ourselves to be, and yet at the same time, know ourselves to be. The amount of psychic energy it takes to deny ourselves to ourselves is massive.

When we walk into the dark forest, all is unleashed, every protection mechanism releases. In my case, the migraine. In others, it might be a different physical illness, panic attacks, a mental health episode, an accident, a separation…

When we allow ourselves to enter the depths of the dark woods our own strange symbols emerge to guide us home to our Self: our own native language. The soul stirs in response. The libido is aroused. Our life force rises in longing. Creativity is unleashed. Boredom evaporates. We feel ourselves fully alive, connected to something timeless within, something strong and strange, and no longer detached from the world, but having, finally found a sense of belonging.

Inner and outer connect.

At last.

"It is possible that archetypes have their own agendas, their own work to do on us."

Kim Krans, *The Wild Unknown Archetype Guidebook*

# The Crow Headed Woman

*"In 2017 I was working full time in two different jobs. I felt as though I had extinguished any idea of purpose or what mine was. I had two children, one of whom was a breastfeeding one year old. My own creativity had been buried under a job, domesticity and caring. Recently I had read Eckhart Tolle's* A New Earth. *A take-away from this was to be more mindful in my day-to-day routines. On my way to work I would walk through an urban city centre park. I initiated a practice of being energetically aware of my feet as I walked and to observe my surroundings: the bird song, the trees, buds emerging, that flower finally bloomed, the changing seasons… I would walk slowly and observe my thoughts but let them flicker away on the breeze.*

*Something emerged from that period. I had always meditated on and off but with no real accountability. After a period of this practice an image of me wearing a giant corvid head appeared in my mind. Some part of me connected or felt an intense gut reaction. When I was in the park the image kept dropping into my internal vision. I put it aside like so many other parts of me. But it came back stronger. 'Take notice of me!'*

*When I thought about crows, rooks, ravens — those carrion creatures who are brave, bold, feisty and clever — they seemed quite different to me, at the time. I was often described as 'nice', and I resisted any form of conflict where possible. In January 2018 I drew my first sketch of a woman with a raven or rook head I wasn't entirely sure which corvid member it was. I had a stomach bug and was sitting in bed feeling poorly and yet that virus gave me time out from my day-to-day activities so I could draw. That tiny drawing in a notebook became a print, a business card and spurred my own creativity and I now make my living as an artist.*

*It took some time for me to understand what the image being presented to me meant. When I thought about the energy of the crow - which is fierce, no nonsense, industrious, independent and has the ability to stand its ground in conflict - they were all attributes I needed to learn. Sometimes, I would leave the house and pretend to wear the crow head as a form of protection. In some way there was an embodiment of the crow. In 2020 I made a drawing of a woman holding a crow head under her arm, with a fox watching. At that point I felt that I had gained some of the crow qualities, as though I no longer needed to wear the crow head myself."*

**Enagh Farrell**

# Dreaming of Wings

I dream of wings.

I dream of a dear old friend, a surrogate grandmother who died whilst I was writing this book. In the dream she is still alive and asking for her mother's wings. I go to the Otherworld and get the wings from her mother: large, feathered, beautiful. She finds comfort in them. I take such pleasure in being in her presence once more. Then suddenly my grandfather and another man I don't know (both of whom are also dead) appear and take the wings back to the Otherworld.

The dream ends.

Other dreams follow. Of wild birds attacked by something unseen, feathers torn from their wings and strewn on the ground.

The death of a man in the community.

Black feathers fall.

# A Gift of Wings

I come down one morning to find a wing in the centre of my kitchen floor.

Or rather, I come down one morning so preoccupied by my thoughts that I do not see the wing at the centre of the kitchen floor, until my cat starts lying next to it, purring and touching it with his paw. Normally feathers are his favourite toy, he rips them apart. This was different. This was a gift. For me. He wanted me to see it and receive it.

*What does this mean?* I wonder.

I salt the wing to preserve it, knowing that feathers and wings are used in ritual the world over: to bless folks with water, waft smoke to cast sacred space, worn as ceremonial attire and placed on altar spaces.

But having preserved the wing, I do not use it. Something in me resists strongly.

I find myself repeating this pattern of behaviour again and again as I move towards embodying the longings I have identified: making a frame drum at a workshop, but then being too afraid to play it. Purchasing another, resisting using it again. Buying a cloak, but being too afraid to put it on. Organising a women's ritual circle and then getting too anxious and cancelling it. I was able to recognise these tools and symbols theoretically, but when it came to visibly embodying them, I froze.

*Why?*

I know that it is no coincidence, the appearance of this wing, at this moment.

Its meaning is not lost on me. It is time to find my own wings. To step fully into my new iteration. My shoulder blades are tight and knotted, I can feel my wings wanting to unfurl.

The thought still terrifies me.

*What will it take?*

*How might it look?*

My whole body tingles at the possibility.

I do not feel safe. This world can be harsh, can be cruel, can be dangerous to edge-dwellers, outsiders.

We have learnt this generation after generation.

Fit in or

Be stoned like the crows.

Be burned like the witches.

Be laughed at or ridiculed by the village.

Be shunned or shamed.

At first glance our fear of other ways of being might seem like overreactions, but look closer and you will see traumas so vast we can barely comprehend. The torture and killing of millions of people who shared their experiences of wild revelation. Who dared to practice their own sacred ways. Who knew themselves as connected to the earth.

This left a scar on the land, and fear in the hearts of generations untold. Its legacy was calculated: a total disconnection from the places we live, from the earth. A distrust of wild revelation, of messages on the wings of crows and in the trees. A fear of what it means if we hear voices or see visions. A fear of our rightness, and a blind compliance with their rules.

Today the tiny pockets of what were once vast rich forests of diverse species are a last trauma wound. A reminder of what once was, and of what has been lost when the native human soul was pushed into the shadows.

"We were not there when women were accused of being crows and messengers from hell, we were neither the judge nor the accused, but we carry these things with us we have to fight them. The best way to do this is to be who you are. Every part of you the good and the bad, the sorrowful and the joyous, you can never run away. There is nowhere to run to."

Alice Hoffman, *The Rules of Magic*

# Ancient Bird Woman

Long before Him, there was Her. Before God there was Goddess.

Before monotheism and a man nailed to a cross. Before the holy spirit coming down as a dove. Before a man finding enlightenment beneath the bodhi tree. Before the many sun gods… there She was.

The divine depicted as bird. As woman. Bird Woman.

The first statues we have are from 20,000 years ago. 18,000 years before the birth of the religion that has come to dominate my homeland and probably yours. A winged woman: the bird goddess.

This is just one of the places the bird goddess was found. She is present in megalithic tombs in the Orkney Islands, France, Portugal, Denmark, Greece, Sweden… [18] She is found in Irish myth as the triple crow goddess The Morrigan: Badh (meaning crow), Neman and Macha.

Ragana, from Lithuania, was goddess of death and regeneration. Like so many she was "degraded to a witch and pushed deep into the forest during the Christian era […] The name Ragana derives from the verb *regėti*, meaning 'to see,' 'to perceive,' 'to divine,' or 'to foresee.' The Lithuanian word *ragas*, 'horn,' as in *ragas mėnulio*, 'moon's horn,' 'crescent moon,' suggests Ragana's relationship with the moon, regeneration, and transformation. She can become a crow, a magpie, a swallow, or a quail, can change her shape into any animate or inanimate form." [19]

The crow goddess brings the message of death. But we have forgotten that after death comes birth once more. Christianity shifted this resurrection onto the body of one divine man, and the promise for true believers to receive it after death, if they follow all the rules here on Earth. But before him the bird goddess – she with wings to ascend, she who walks the Earth, she the layer of eggs – taught us of regeneration.

"One of the Goddess's archaic forms,
the crone Coronis, was a crow."

Barbara G. Walker,
*The Woman's Book of Symbols and Sacred Objects*

Before the churches and temples, there were Her sacred groves. The places dedicated to She who was linked to the moon. She who flew. She who gave birth to the world. She who women embodied with their life-giving wombs.

But She would not be allowed to co-exist with the new and jealous god.

Her groves were cut, her priestesses and followers demonised: women and trees felled and burned, birds stoned. The living wisdom thread of nature was cut from spiritual practice: the drums silenced, the magic wand snapped, Her symbols erased or subsumed, Her traces buried, Her names forbidden.

We who have come after know of the price to be paid for worshipping at the altar of nature. The danger of wild revelation. The danger of following Her ways and our own hearts in the world of the patriarchs.

And yet over the last century Her symbols have been emerging, thick and fast, from the earth… in the form of long buried statues, long forgotten practices. In the beat of the drum, the movement of the pen and brush, memories of Her are flooding our dreams, initiating us.

We are remembering another way of living.

## The Crow as Healing and Transformation

*"Crows have featured in my maternal lineage for many generations. My great-great-grandmother and all the women before her were speyywives of the Scottish highlands. The speywives were the community healers, clairvoyants and midwives who had herbal knowledge and healing abilities. Their companion animals were said to be black cats or black birds. My great-great-great-grandmother, also a speywife, was said to have had raven black hair, suspiciously, even into her old age until death. In Celtic folklore, the crow is a representation of Cailleach, the Goddess of cold and wind, the divine Hag and the healer."*

**Gemma Clark and Isabel Brady**

# Sacred Grove

I decide to decorate my drum with the image of Crow. Then I don my cloak, bury the good girl in the earth and begin to play.

Time shifts and morphs. A powerful trance state takes me into the dark Self. To the sacred grove within and the heart of the wood.

There I see a circle of women who I met many, many years ago in a powerful dream. Then I was standing outside of the circle, observing. This time I am welcomed in. I stand and introduce myself. Then ask them to introduce themselves to me. Some I know from this lifetime, some I don't.

A strange orgasmic pulse passes through my whole body. My nervous system feels like it is being played as a drum, as a drum skin for Her voice.

I am here.

"The drum was the means our ancestors used to summon the goddess and also the instrument through which she spoke. The drumming priestess was the intermediary between divine and human realms. Aligning herself with sacred rhythms, she acted as summoner and transformer.

In rituals invoking the archetypal pattern of death and rebirth, the drum signaled the release of outmoded behavior patterns and the transition to a new status in life."

Layne Redmond, *When the Drummers Were Women*

# Goddess on the Wing

On the drive home from my women's group, I am transfixed by the bright full moon hanging high over the bay. I drive down to the beach, still wondering how – if – I can finally live out the ways of Bird Woman in my daily life.

I sing to the sea and the stars – "Ancient Mother, I hear you calling". I anoint myself with seawater and give thanks for the day. I head back to the car feeling free and at peace.

I realise as I walk to the car that today was the first anniversary of the release of my book, *She of the Sea*. I have not been able to go to the beach alone since then. It has been a year's cycle. When it launched, I lined up lots of podcasts to speak on to promote the book, but then found myself pretty much unable to mention it – I felt traumatised by the way I had exposed my self that I had hidden so well: my autistic bits, the magic, the witchy goddessy bits... I felt drenched in sticky shame.

I thought about the virtual book club I would be doing on *She of the Sea* in September and how I am ready to speak about it.

At last, at last. It is time.

At this point I was sat in the car. I turned on the headlights and there ahead of me illuminated, was a bird. Not any bird, but an owl, on the lifebuoy stand, looking right back at me.

We held each other's stare, then she spread her wings – wings that brought to mind the one my cat brought me a few weeks ago that I thought belonged to an owl – and then was gone into the darkness.

I have never seen an owl in the wild. I would never expect to see an owl anywhere near the sea! Back at home I googled which owls we have in Ireland – I knew it wasn't a barn owl, and it certainly wasn't a long-eared owl. It was a short-eared owl, rare in Ireland, usually leaving to breed in Russia during the summer, they over-winter here in Ireland but rarely stay year-round. They frequent dunes and coastal areas.

Her appearance at this point in my thought and emotional process felt nothing short of magic: a sign.

The owl is often associated with the sacred feminine, symbol and associate of the Goddess, especially goddesses Athena and Minerva. In Irish mythology she (for she is almost always female in the stories) is associated with the crone, and one of her names is cailleach oidhche – crone of the night.

Throughout European folklore she is a bird commonly associated with witches. Night-flying and wise.

And here she was. Appearing to me at this moment.

Magical and real. Both.

"We all start out knowing magic. We are born with whirlwinds, forest fires, and comets inside us. We are born able to sing to birds and read the clouds and see our destiny in grains of sand. But then we get the magic educated right out of our souls. We get it churched out, spanked out, washed out, and combed out."

Robert McCammon

# Magic

I have used this word magic many times now, but what do I mean by it?

Magic, for me, is a short word for a tricky concept. One that is easy to experience but hard to put into words.

Magic takes up where modern science and philosophy leave off. It floods into every entangled space of being and reveals itself slowly. It requires that we enter into experience embodied and unafraid of the dark and the strange.

Magic has at its heart a livingness, a responsiveness, a reciprocal consciousness that science does not recognise. It allows space for the soul. For transformation beyond logic. For the impossible, the improbable, the longed for. It both allows us – and the universe – more agency. And the possibility of creative collaboration. It has at its heart a web of interbeing that only ecologists and quantum physicists in mainstream culture can really grasp. It embraces the unseen. Without needing to try and see it. It accepts the darkness of mind and logical knowing and embraces the reality of divergent non-repeatable lived experience and revelation.

It is a state of being where we understand the psyche as a vital layer of reality alive in the world. One where we see the realm of symbol as active within and without, and the world as woven from energies which can be mediated, played with, transformed.

To allow for magic is to give space to a greater reality than our current culture can explain or conceptualise. A reality where consciousness affects the material world. One that acknowledges the truth that not only humans are conscious, and where things like time may be far more complex or entirely different than we currently understand.

Magic lives in the margins, on the edges of days, on the perimeters of places, where one threshold crosses or touches another, in the realm of Crow and Moon.

Whenever you enter the wild with openness to the encounter there is the potential to experience magic. This I know as truth.

We re-enter an ever-present living presence, a complex non-human living system, a matrix of symbols. If we allow ourselves to become part of it, we experience a falling away of time – of this time in history and the daily roles we play – and remember a timeless sense of being. We meet the shadow selves that we have as individuals and culture banished to the dark to die, and rediscover ancient forgotten symbols and archetypes that can help us rediscover our own meaning.

I want to live in a world where we take time to attend to the magic unfolding. Where we know how to listen and watch. Within. Without. Where we pray in birds, learn to sing the light into being each morning and dance the stars awake each night, just as they do. Theirs is the song of the liminal. They are the keepers of the space between sky and land, day and night.

This is why we follow the birds
Into the wild places.

Because the feathered ones have never
Lost their connection to the unseen realms.

"Magic is a way of sensing, experiencing, being, magic is a lens that is the body, a place where light passes through and warms us, draws attention, rouses us from feeling and propels us to action."

Sabrina Scott, *Witchbody*

# Is It Real?

We have been warned about these things…
The magical.
The illogical.

The wild.

The unknown.

The supernatural.

We have been warned not to be naïve or credulous, not to allow our feelings to run away with us. We have been told not to follow every impulse that flits through our bodies, or believe every thought that crosses our minds.

We have been taught to be cynical and sceptical. To be rational.

And so, naturally, there is a moment when reality as we know it shifts and magic emerges that we question what has just happened.

Because lived spiritual experience is so little spoken of outside of religious circles, we may doubt ourselves and our experiences. Is this new/ancient place we entered real or imaginary? Is it the product of our own delusional minds? Is it a psychotic break or wishful thinking? Or are we experiencing a truer reality?

Who or what can we trust?

What can we believe?

The mind circles. Logic falters. Words fail. The body, however, knows. The psyche streams out images in response.

"There is a world beyond ours... That world talks.
It has a language of its own."[20]

Maria Sabina

# Squaring the Circle

Squaring the circle refers to an attempt do something impossible.

In the context of my journey, this to me means being able to embody the two realities in which I find myself: the energetic, unseen realms of soul, the unconscious, the magical and the realm of my logical, modern mind. To embody the values of feminine and masculine. To find a way for the wild and the modern to co-exist. To navigate and value the inner and outer worlds, and find a way to weave them together into one body, one life. This is the challenge that all of us who walk this path face: of reclaiming and staying connected to authentic soulful practice within the crumbling ruins of the modern materialist world and rationalist philosophy in which we were raised.

What is exciting is that this is happening on an individual and collective level at the same time. I am not – you are not – alone in this experience.

We are finding our way back to the roots of an authentic human spiritual expression, arising from our deepest longings for belonging and connection to ourselves, to each other and to the natural world. One which honours and is led by our personal and collective symbology, rather than the second-hand spirituality which has been forced upon populations for millennia through guilt, shame, violence and a need to conform. Simultaneously we are rediscovering a far deeper way of belonging to this Earth, necessary not only for our own mental and physical wellbeing but for the survival of our species.

Some of us are taught and initiated by teachers, but many of us aren't. When we lack an outer guide to how to proceed, our inner images and symbols spring up to assist us in navigating this tumultuous upheaval: the psyche and the wild are in cahoots on this one. Their aims are united, the evolutionary push of consciousness and life force are one and the same. All we have to do is allow them.

I realised, as I reflected on the images that came through me, that Crow could be seen as symbolising our animal self, and the Moon the sacred. Together they represent the desire for unity, our longing to fly into intimate relationship with the sacred. This is and has always been a basic human urge – to reconcile our animal and sacred aspects, to find wholeness, self-understanding and deep belonging.

Each generation of Western culture has lived further and further detached from the natural world: both literally and philosophically, the gap between ourselves and the natural world has grown, until we no longer see ourselves as part of it. Or it as part of us.

Any wild initiation is an invitation to us as individuals to do what our culture is yet unable to do collectively: to heal the split that Western culture has perpetuated through our own lived experience. To reconcile for ourselves the division of matter from consciousness, and reject the peculiar insistence that the world is made of two things: the material – treated as the real, usually considered inanimate, and the psycho-spiritual – which troubles us greatly as we still cannot see, touch or taste it, nor say exactly what this is.

As we first begin to improvise authentic spiritual practice for ourselves we may feel strange – and look strange to others – because we live in a culture that has moved so far from weaving the sacred into everyday actions, that we do look very different to the rest of our culture when we choose to do this.

Religion since its beginnings has been a collective act. That is why it can be so hard to leave the religion of our youth behind and why we can feel so self-conscious attempting to create and evolve a more meaningful, personal spiritual practice for ourselves. It is why we can be deeply worried about standing out from the crowd. Spiritual acts are strange and powerful, and doing them alone can make us into an easy target for the discomfort of others, whereas when we are able to practice together, both our sense of safety, but also our spiritual power increases.

Crow teaches us that there is power in numbers. When we square the circle together, magic happens. Consciousness shifts on the collective level.

# Crow Medicine

*"During many years of spiritual searching studying Celtic indigenous rituals and practices… my guiding presence was and still is a great black bird who possesses a penetrating all-seeing eye. Starting any meditative journey, I stare into her dark abyss to seek permission and guidance to cross over into liminal spaces. Knowing and naming this as 'The Morrigan' seems too prescriptive, too simple for this powerful medicine, which supports me as I place my trust in the unknown, the mystical, which brings deep intuitive ancestral healing."*

**Barbara O'Meara**

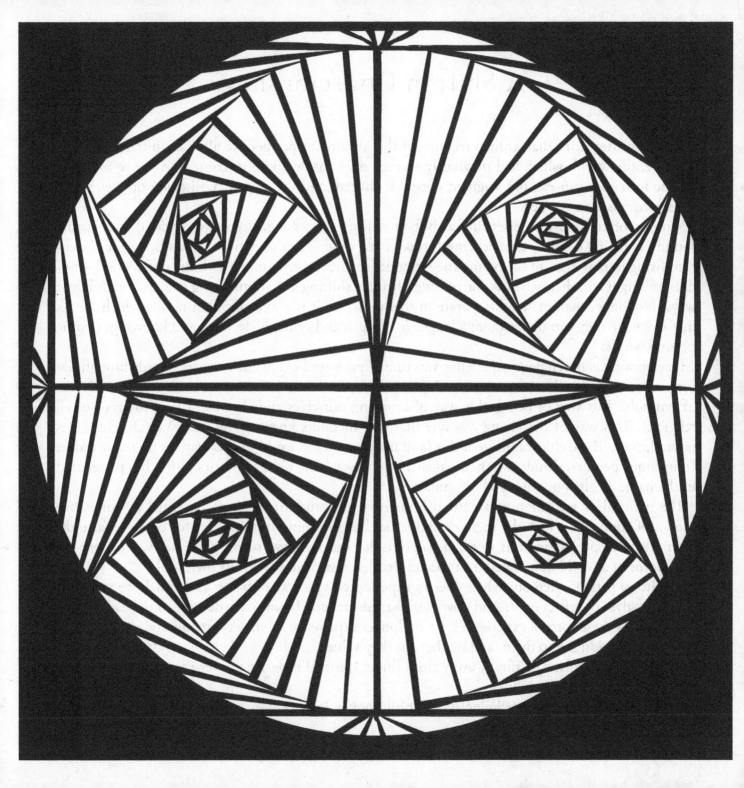

# A Shift in Consciousness

In story after story that women recount of this shifting of perspective after an initiatory experience, the world, which had previously seemed dead inside and out, comes alive once more. In the initiatory process, old stagnant energy is shifted, and the ancient wellspring of energy and consciousness is uncovered.

Women often report experiencing a shift in sensory processing, becoming synaesthetic: tasting sounds, smelling colours, experiencing forms as less solid. Their awareness expands, a sign of neurons firing in new areas of the brain. They experience direct communion with the outer world – understanding it and themselves as one pulsing life force shifting and shimmering in a million different ways. No longer inanimate nor separate to them, instead it is a web of pulsating life which speaks in a language they can understand: a language of signs and symbols, feelings and knowings that lie beyond words.

Pre-monotheism, religious experience was one of profound connection to the sacred through nature. It was – and still is – a path of both personal revelation and collective ritual, a wild revelation of symbols. This way of being, this way of knowing ourselves and the world is at the root of all religions. This way of perceiving was one that our ancestors knew as the only way of being. It is natural to us. The Celtic tradition of this land understood the world in this way. As do many today: Indigenous peoples, druids, witches, pagans, priestesses… the ones Western culture has persecuted in the name of 'the one true God' for millennia.

The removal of revelation as a natural human faculty, and art-making and ritual as our native modes of connection with the mystery of life, has had profound implications for ourselves as individuals and a species, and our world. Look outside your window, turn on the news, these are the symptoms of a world dominated by a species that has lost contact with its own soul.

The irony is that when our whole species experienced this way of being as normal, we were not able to analyse or reflect on it. And now that our cultures and brains have developed to be able to be conscious of these sorts of experiences, we no longer experience them very frequently: our culture is simply not conducive to them, and neither are they valued.

We may have evolved culturally away from direct spiritual experience over the past few hundred years, but we retain our abilities.

Mid-twentieth century psychologist and philosopher Jean Gebser referred to this "primitive"[21] form of consciousness as "magical". But he stresses that it did not just disappear as other "higher" forms of consciousness (which enable rational thought or self-awareness) developed. Gebser asserted that we can integrate previous layers of consciousness – archaic, magical, mythic and mental – to create what he called Integral Consciousness: one that is able both to function in our modern technological realm, process ideas and sensory input using rational thought and advanced skills, and at the same time maintain our ability to perceive and connect with the symbolic, magical realms. We have the capacity to square the circle.

This potential for integrated ways of knowing, seeing and understanding ourselves and the world is innate to us, lying dormant within each of us. Just below the surface. Magical consciousness can be switched on instantaneously through certain drugs, in active imagination, trance states, meditation, lucid dreams, out-of-body and near-death experiences, and the initiatory experiences that we have been exploring here. And, even more excitingly, when we begin to regularly engage with this mode of consciousness – through creativity, active imagination, dreamwork – our skillfulness increases, our awareness increases, and we find any ever-growing symbiosis between our inner and outer worlds.

When we learn to see again with magical consciousness, the imaginal space of symbols becomes overlaid on and through the daily world. Life begins to have meaning again. We begin to know the world as our home, as a material and spiritual reality. We can inhabit both. We can square the circle.

For a while in the twentieth century, it seemed as though this capacity was on the verge of becoming a widespread possibility for our species, as men in many fields tried to probe the boundaries of human experience with the tools of science, art, philosophy, psychedelics and spirituality.

Father of psychoanalysis Sigmund Freud, wrote of the importance of dreams and the unconscious mind, and his one-time collaborator, and founder of analytic psychology, C.G. Jung explored the collective unconscious, the shadow and archetypal realm, synchronicity, using active imagination, mandalas and art-making as ways of accessing these.

Surrealist artists showed a world of man-made objects morphing and metamorphosing with the natural world and the absurdity of the material world when played with by the human mind.

Aleister Crowley and Gerald Gardner set out the frameworks of modern witchcraft.

Meditation in many forms – yoga, Transcendental Meditation, Zazen, Vipassana, Chi Gung, mindfulness – reached the masses through great male teachers: B.K.S. Iyengar, S.N. Goenka, Ram Dass, the Maharishi, Jon-Kabat-Zinn, Thich Nhat Hanh.

Hungarian-American psychologist Mihaly Csikszentmihalyi wrote of flow and peak experiences.

British author Aldous Huxley opened the doors of perception by taking the psychedelic drug mescalin and wrote of his experiences. Academics, psychiatrists and hippies explored the hidden realms

of consciousness using LSD, Ecstasy, magic mushrooms, marijuana…

Each was exploring different modes of consciousness experienced by humans throughout our history, native to us all, but left out of our self-understanding through the Western focus on the rational mind and the pre-frontal cortex. These modes of consciousness which have been buried in the collective shadow for so long were finally, finally being taken seriously. Albeit through the lens of male bodies, minds and pens.

The doors were flung wide open, and we teetered on the edge, ready to fly into the future with this new understanding of our native human powers. Human abilities, which had previously been misunderstood or ignored were gathering credence – deep relaxation, remote viewing, psychokinesis, mind reading – were being investigated, shared and discussed. Secretive projects run by state agencies such as the CIA, KGB and Nazis tried to see if these powers could be harnessed for patriarchal aims, in war and domination.

And then the door slammed shut again, as laws were passed against psychedelics, wars were started using ever darker psychological techniques, inflation rose, fear ratcheted up, the pace of life increased, the climate crisis emerged. The Western world went back to business as usual, ignoring the progress of the modern prophets, the revelations of our full human capacities, the dark mysteries of the psyche, and pushing them firmly back into the shadow, shutting down or shaming anyone who chose to take this path alone. Leaving a taste of fear where there should be magic.

"Whatever the unconscious may be, it is a natural phenomenon producing symbols that prove to be meaningful."

C.G. Jung, *Man and his Symbols*

# Dark Gifts

And so here we are, intrepid explorers, branching out on our own, in a world that is going crazy yet claims itself sane.

The dark woods act as repositories for the states of consciousness that are little used in our culture. The hidden gifts we have disowned. The skills that are not needed. The ways of knowing and being that have been denied. The gifts that are our birthright.

High sensitivity.

Awareness of unseen energies.

Seeing visions.

Ability to enter trance.

Receiving revelation.

Foretelling the future.

Reading minds.

Healing with hands.

Speaking with nature.

Gifts of spiritual flight.

Shapeshifting abilities.

Direct engagement with the Otherworld.

Communing with spirits.

We have no role for humans with these gifts in Western culture. We deny their reality because we do not understand it. But they are ancient human faculties: every culture in human history has acknowledged them, some have accepted them.

In other cultures, in other times those who possess these dark gifts were called:

Seer, Medicine person, Shaman, Oracle, Artist, Healer, Priestess, Sorceress…

We scorn these titles and realities, and instead we have learned to call the one that shows these dark gifts.

Mad

Crazy

Witch.

"Life itself initiates each of us according to our own peculiar stories. Our stories lead us toward our purpose in this world. Each initiation strips something away and gives us a gift. If we want to meet our full form, we are obligated to give that gift to the world."

Amanda Yates Garcia, *Initiated*

# Different Does not Equal Bad

*"The crows have been talking to me more lately, and they have been talking in earnest. They are waiting for me when I go outside; flying overhead or by a window just a heartbeat after I look up. Looking at me with a knowing. Beckoning and allowing me to step closer than most people are allowed.*

*I see the crows get harassed by smaller birds. Yes, I feel empathy for the crows. They are only trying to do their thing, live their lives. The crows eat the eggs and nestlings of the smaller birds, but that doesn't mean that they are bad or evil. It is a part of the natural order of things. Death feeds life, feeds death, feeds life… Good, bad, negative, indifferent. These are all labels based on preconceived and biased notions about the world around us.*

*Different does not equal bad; it is an opportunity to shift perception. I've never felt like I fit in and have been more of an observer than a participant throughout my life. This has allowed me to have a different perspective and my observations tend to challenge the established biases. As a result, they aren't always welcome, but they are there. Take them or leave them. Let them simmer a bit in your subconscious until something unravels inside. Or follow me into the mystery, into the journey of unknowing. The beginner's mind is crucial in everything we do, including understanding ourselves.*

*To know yourself, you must first unknow yourself.*

*As someone who walks the edges and blazes a path slightly ahead of others, it is easy to feel lost or not well-received. The creative process might just be the catalyst for my own personal unknowing. My own return to a beginner's mind.*

*So, the crows keep talking to me and following me. Even as they are being harassed, they speak to me. 'Keep doing what you are doing. Your art, your medicine are important. Affecting change is not easy but keep doing what you are doing.' Step into Crow's message with me. Walk along this mystical path of unknowing so that we can all learn to know ourselves and each other again."*

**Megan Desrosiers**

# An Archetype Emerges

I tried to keep the Witch out of this book… in order to make it safe. For me. For you.

Because for every woman who thrills to see the archetype of Witch and runs towards it with open arms and mind, knowing her to be a wise woman, there are countless more who hear Witch, smell smoke and run and hide. For fear of what if.

I resisted her emergence. In the book. In myself.

Because she scared me.

Because I wanted to be taken seriously.

And patriarchal culture does not take the Witch seriously. As I wrote in *Burning Woman:*

"Want to discredit a woman in the real world? All you need is one word.

Witch. Still. In the 21st century."

The Witch is the antithesis of patriarchy.

She represents the dark. The feminine. The magical. The irrational.

They do not admit her wisdom or her ways of working.

They do not admit her reality.

Yet still, she emerges. In our world, in ourselves. Unbidden.

"Archetypes appear in practical experience: They are, at the same time, both images and emotions... Being charged with emotion, the image gains psychic energy, it becomes dynamic, and consequences of some kind must flow from it."

C.G. Jung, *Man and his Symbols*

"Every hurt, every wound, pushed the witch in her further and further into the hinterlands, the dark woods of her psyche. [...] As a child, she always wanted to feel normal, to feel ordinary. [...] Ordinary meant safe. [...] By her early thirties, the witch in [her] had gone dormant. She was exhausted. Her struggles [...] had sucked her oceans dry. And for a while she thought if she could just be that perfect woman, wife, mother, daughter, be beautiful and kind and not complain, then things might get easier for her. But then, when things did get easier and her life stabilized, like a plant in your garden some call medicine and others call a weed, the witch in her came flowering back."

Amanda Yates Garcia, *Initiated*

There are many witches: wicked witches of storybooks; real people put to death by Christian witch-hunters; people who have gifts and proclivities that would have had them accused of practicing witchcraft; and the edge-dwellers – artists, poets, seers, healers, psychics, mediums – who have always been viewed with suspicion because how they work and what they do is incomprehensible and inconceivable to the mainstream Western mind.

We are taught to be scared of all these witches, their strangeness, their power. We have learned to scorn, deny and denounce the Witch wherever we may find her, if we are to be a good girl of the patriarchy. Just as we have learned to disown any element of ourselves that could be associated with the Witch. Something I followed even in my own book as I saw her emerging in my images, in myself. Because I know how dangerous she can be.

And so, my psyche made her safer for me. It masked her. Allowed me to see her as Bird Woman, my muse and alter-ego first. Allowed me to remember her herstory as Bird Goddess.

But *Crow Moon* wasn't *Crow Moon* without the Witch.

This was her realm: the dark woods, the crow, magic, mushrooms, the moon, death, times of change and transformation…

The Witch demanded to be seen. To be heard. As she was, as she is. Here. Now. Unmasked.

"[The Witch] brings us to our true nature. She breaks stasis, or purposefully creates it. She sets things in motion, stirs the pot, is instigator and matrix of fateful odysseys and transformations. [...] She is also the weird earth of our restoration. She makes things so intolerable that we are forced to break the lock. She scares the life into us."

*The Book of Symbols*

I am witch!
My power has been denied, decried
Yet still I am here!
I am witch!
I have been burned and caged
Yet still I am here!
I fly, I defy
I see
With my eyes.
I cannot be contained or constrained
For I am witch!
I live as I wish
I do as I will
I speak as I choose
I bow to none
I am witch!

"Flying the night skies of psyche, the Witch brings primordial realities into culture's brittle convictions. Like all aspects of the collective unconscious, the Witch lays low when times are fine but rises when times are tense."

This Jungian Life,
"The Archetype of the Witch"

In Jungian psychology the archetype of the Witch tends to come to prominence at midlife, as the childrearing years fade away and crow's feet begin to appear around our eyes, the wise woman, the crone – crow woman – emerges from within.

The Witch archetype is an energy force that moves powerfully through us, just like the many other archetypes that arise over the course of our lifetimes: Daughter, Mother, Healer, Teacher… But unlike these others she holds enormous negative charge with her – culturally and internally. She brings with her the hungry ghosts of all the shadow selves we have denied. She comes demanding to be seen and heard by a world that does not, will not, cannot accept her. She comes to stir the cauldron at the centre of our being.

You know the Witch, though you may deny it. You know her energy. You recognise her embodiments.

The Witch is a marginal woman, she of liminal spaces. She is probably the sort of woman you were warned against as a child.

She is the woman with the wild look in her eye who might curse you. The one who lived alone in a strange house at the edge of a village that you would run fast past with your breath held. The woman who intrigued you, who seemed to dance to her own inner drum and be animated by something more than the other adults. The one who made images or spoke to spirits. The one who fed the birds or had a house full of cats. The one who dressed for herself. Who sang at the top of her voice and muttered to herself as she walked down the street. She who followed her own rules and gave the one fingered salute to the patriarchs.

The witch is one who lives on her own terms, sees the hypocrisy of our culture for what it is, and calls it out.

She who is not living afraid of death.

She who is not afraid of her own shadow.

She who speaks up.

She who is wild.

She who is wise.

She who is free.

"The witch image depicts the force that arises when women want to create themselves and from themselves in ways other than biological reproduction. [...] The witch figure presents an awesome image of the primordial feminine concerned with herself. [...] life flows inward and downward to feed the deep recesses of a woman's psyche [...] out of consciousness and into unconsciousness. [...] To go where the witch leads is to discover that the opposites contain their opposites that the rational hides an irrationality and that the irrational hides a hidden logic."

Ann and Barry Ulanov, *The Witch and the Clown*

It is important to stress that just because the archetype of Witch emerges within you, does not mean you have to suddenly identify as a witch. Unless, of course, you want to!

As with any archetype, the more you struggle with the archetype of Witch, and deny or repress her emergence, perhaps due to religious affiliation or your upbringing, the harder the journey with her will be. Like any emergent archetype, the Witch asks certain questions of us at a critical juncture of our psychological development. She emerges unbidden, requiring us to express hidden parts of ourselves, bringing new facets of our personality to light, drawing our attention to herself through new art, books or films that contain depictions of her. She – the forbidden woman – comes alive for us in ourselves…and in the world.

The gift of the archetype of the Witch is to help us to navigate the dark woods of the unconscious and work magic with what we find there. She is our guide on this journey of midlife reclamation.

She who has been burned, names herself,

Claims herself

Claims her spiritual authority

And commits to life

On her own terms.

At last.

"The etymology of the word witch comes from the German *hexe*, which actually means fence. And the word *hag* also means fence. So, witches were fence riders, they are creatures that live on the border between two things. We could imagine that they also exist on this border between the human and the divine, human and the demonic, conscious and the unconscious... In some cultures, artists are considered dangerous almost as if they're witches and in cultures that are controlled by highly fascist governments artists are arrested, controlled, or they're made to disappear because they're introducing something new into the culture, something of the unconscious into the culture. The modern witch can be the artist, writer, poet, anything that stirs the soul in a way that honors the unconscious, challenges the status quo. They are fence riding people of the world."

This Jungian Life, "The Archetype of the Witch"

# Hidden Magic

"*Our family ranch sits nestled within the foothills of Alberta, a stone's throw away from the majestic Rockies.*

*This territory is home to dinosaur-like ravens.*

*I was in my roaring twenties, dabbling in waves of self-deception and hiding from my power and magic. I was on the way to meet an ex-boyfriend in town, one who despite his desire for me, was not the one. I felt a sense of danger as I sped along the country highway; in my head and disconnected from nature's messages of warning. Out of nowhere, a raven intercepted my path and flew right into my windshield. A shockwave of shame slammed into me as I stomped on the brakes and jumped into the middle of the gravel road. The raven was nowhere to be seen. There was no dead raven anywhere.*

*I found myself on this same country road with my brother and sister-in-law. Once again, I was navigating disruption in my life. I had begun to work with the Runes and embrace my gift as a Medium and channel for the dead. My sister-in-law was driving, and she slammed on the brakes. A swarm of ravens flew directly in front of our windshield; encased within their circle was an eagle. The light was being wrangled by the dark. An unlikely scene, reminding me that my magic depended on my darkness and the unseen parts of me. It was time to stop hiding.*"

**Chloe Elgar**

# A Witch is One...

A witch is one who looks at the world

And comes to a different conclusion

to the one, she has been taught.

A witch is one

Who lives into her questions

And answers to no one.

A witch is one

Who takes the power into her own hands

And conjures her own destiny.

Who builds her own drum

And lives to the beat of it.

A witch is one

Who is not afraid of the dark.

A witch is one

who can speak to the animals,

understand the trees,

reads the winds like a book,

and the stars as a map.

A witch is one

who sees beyond, beneath, behind.

A witch is one

who knows what it means to be burned

And to rise.

A witch is one

who knows wildness and will not be tamed.

A witch is one

who knows her way

To the heart of the dark woods

And finds herself at home there.

A witch is one

who weaves webs between the worlds.

Keeper of the wild spaces

Traveller of the dark earth.

Agent of change.

A witch is one who enchants the world.

Her cape woven of the threads of old stories

And the sparkle of new beginnings.

A witch is one who follows the way of the crow

And lives by moon light.

A witch is one

But many.

OOO

I breathe this knowing into my body.

Let it weave through my nervous system.

Until it becomes integral to my very core

May this shifting in my vision and hearing

Remain as the pain disperses and daily life resumes.

Let it settle into my bones

Circulate in my blood

Infuse into my soul

Until I am one with this knowing

Until it is me

And I it

Inseparable, entwined.

"A real witch knows who she is and
what she can do and does it."

This Jungian Life, "The Archetype of the Witch"

# Shapeshifter

*"Cloaked in black, she steps out at twilight. Veiled by thick nocturnal mist. Dark stockings and sturdy boots protrude from beneath the ragged hem. Unnoticed, her power under wraps, until the first gust of wind ruffles her luminous black feathers. She fills her lungs with the night's cold breath. Feels a surge. Stifles the urge to caw until the costume change is complete, trading her boots for claws, her wool for wings. She is not of this world. Descended from the stars. Once a month she takes flight. Silhouette against the moon. Heralding another cycle of life, death, rebirth."*

**Janet Lucy**

ooo

*"The crow in me sees the crow in you — this is a remembrance; in the rafters of our hearts sits a holy crow, preening its feathers, ready to take flight."*

**Alexandra de Angelis**

# Women of the Crow

At these moments of archetypal emergence, transformation and wild revelation we can often feel alone, especially if we look to mainstream culture for guidance or reassurance. We may feel as though we are going crazy.

But we are not.

This ongoing initiation into the feminine, this psychic development, is normal and natural. We are becoming whole, more real than we have ever allowed ourselves to be before. We are living on purpose in the midst of a culture which requires conformity and superficiality over authenticity and connection.

The Bird Woman, the Witch, those who are taken by the crows in midlife… we are many. We are finding our way off the path of a broken culture and co-creating something new and ancient, here and now, apart but together.

But this reality is hidden in the mainstream. Just as it always has been.

Most women's stories of psychological, spiritual and creative development have been disregarded, hidden, silenced or ridiculed throughout patriarchy. Their importance denied. Often it takes years until we come to the realisation that the vast majority of the experiences of spiritual awakening we have heard, have been those of men. Most of the insights of nature both literal and symbolic have been shared by the pens of men. Most of the voices of art and religion, myth and poetry that honoured the ways of the crow were the voices of our forefathers – Ted Hughes, Charles Dickens, Odin and Apollo, those who wrote our fairy tales, who defined what it means to be a witch in fiction and actuality – were male. We have been fed the words and images of men, and been starved of the voices, revelations and experiences of women, as though they didn't matter, didn't differ.

I believe that the voices which are missing, the voices that centred feminine and female experiences, are the ones we need now, more than ever. As individuals. As a collective. There is a gaping void where they should be: the voices of the bird women, daughters of the crow. The women who have discovered their own language of symbols. The women who found their way home to themselves on the wings of birds. The women who dared to reach beyond how they were told to see the world, to claim their own voices, their own visions.

"It is especially important for women to learn more about the language of symbols, because many common religious symbols were stolen from ancient woman-centered systems and reinterpreted in the contexts of patriarchy. As women struggle out from under centuries of patriarchal oppression, they find it necessary to reclaim their symbols and reapply them to feminine interests. [...] While it is true that symbols are whatever one cares to make of them, it is also true that Western civilization's symbolism has gone in directions that ignore or belittle the female principle."

Barbara G. Walker,
*The Woman's Book of Symbols and Sacred Objects*

Throughout the pages of this book, I have shared not only my own story, but the stories and experiences of many other women who have found their wisdom on the wings of crows. We are just some. I want to share a few more here, as breadcrumbs for your path, so that you can begin to unearth your own sisterhood of soul and feather your own wisdom path.

I commend to you the strange and wonderful surrealist art of British-Mexican artist Leonora Carrington. The life of Simona Kossak, an ecologist who lived deep in the Polish woods with her "terrorist crow", sharing her bed with a lynx.[22] Artist and author Audrey Niffenegger and her modern fairy tale of *Raven Girl,* which became a ballet. Meinread Craighead, Christian mystic and visionary and her primal images of Crow Mother. Psychotherapists Sharon Blackie and Virginia Beane Rutter with their insights on the mythopoetic and the feminine and Cali White, organiser of The Witches' Revival. Authors and podcast hosts Amanda Yates Garcia, Risa Dickens and Amy Torok (Missing Witches), Pam Grossman, and all the many other women and witches digging back into our history and art and pointing out the rich lineage of wise women and magic that have been hidden. I urge you to seek them out.

The connection between spirituality and creativity is one that has been lost in our culture. So many of these women are reconnecting the interweaving threads, insisting that one is an integral part of the other. Both are inspired acts, ways of tapping into something greater than ourselves, some sort of intelligence that we cannot fully grasp or understand with our minds, yet, through these acts, we embody them, closing the aching gap between ourselves and the sacred.

As I wrote, I realised that the desire to silence or ignore the voice of woman and the voice of crow are connected. For both call to other ways of being, other ways of seeing, other realities, out beyond the walls of patriarchy. They speak in the voice of the dark woods that unsettles the certainty of the patriarchal myth, and bring forth ancient wisdom and dark gifts, if we will only have the courage to receive them.

# Raven by Name

"Several years ago, I decided to select a pen name for my creative projects. I am a writer, an artist and a singer/songwriter. I planned to keep the name Hunter because that is my maiden name and I like it. Near my birthday, I did a card reading using the Medicine Cards.

The first card I drew from the deck was number 16. I thought how auspicious because I was born on the 16th day of the year. The card was Raven. The information about Raven said, 'Throughout time, Raven has carried the medicine of Magic.' It also explained that Raven is the messenger of the Great Mystery and ceremonial magic and healing. I took this card as a sign and created my pen name, Raven Hunter.

I later added the middle initial of S. Raven S Hunter, the feminine form of Raven, Raven-ess. Naming myself was empowering.

Within several weeks of deciding on my new creative name, two ravens came to stay in the large juniper trees in front of our house. They soon began to land on our roof and the front porch. We gave them treats and their favorite was graham crackers.

Eventually, they knocked on the windows with their beaks to get our attention. We threw graham crackers into the air, and they swooped down from the trees or the roof to catch them with their beaks. When I took walks up the hill, they flew above me.

I named the ravens Magic and Mystery. They stayed with us for about a month and then one day they flew off into the blue New Mexico sky. They were an affirmation for me. To this day, Raven has continued to be my magical pen name, totem and a guide in my life."

**Raven S Hunter**

# Predator Mother

*"I am a Dutch artist working with the indigenous Frisian goddess Baduhenna. I perceive her as a Great Corvid, a Predator Mother.*

*Roman writer Tacitus described the Battle of Baduhenna Wood, where the Frisians attack the Roman invaders, in a spirit of battle frenzy.*

*I started working with Baduhenna on a solitary forest retreat in Sweden. I created her an altar, intuitively choosing items such as feathers and a raven mask. Once darkness cloaked the house, I lit candles and spoke prayers. I danced to invoke her. Soon it felt like I was dancing inside her; that she was a great corvid who had feasted on me. This was not frightening but deeply reassuring because it connected me to the great cycle of Life-Death-Rebirth.*

*For one week I kept my attention on Baduhenna 24/7. One night a bird kept me awake, rustling under the roof over my bedroom. This brought the sensation of sleeping in the nest of a Predator Mother, who won't hesitate to kill in order to feed me. The price for her tender care is the insight that one day I too (or least my corpse) will become food for hungry beings other than myself. This is the deal for all children of the Mother Goddess, by necessity also a Death Goddess.*

*I went foraging and I found her a bright blue mushroom and red berries from a rowan tree, to represent drops of blood on her altar.*

*The next morning, I was up before sunrise and made my way to the lake. Two ravens kept me company. One sat in the top of a pine tree, calling out to all directions. The other one circled the lake a few times, flying right over my head. When Sunna (the sun, personified as a female giantess in Norse cosmology) rose over the lake, both shrieked loudly and flew off. Their job was done. I assumed they were Huginn and Muninn, Odin's ravens!*

*Back home Baduhenna started appearing in my paintings. I felt a desire to carve her name into rock, using the runes of the Frisian Futhark, so she would not slide into oblivion. I don't think she would handle oblivion well – she might shape-shift into an even more ferocious bird and come for us, if she does not receive her allocated share."*

**Imelda Almqvist**

# Spring

My migraines begin to dissipate as the book draws to a close, and I return to the woods. To the outside world it is as though none of my pain has happened. None of my travails in the dark woods within are visible here. The trees do not know the darkness I have felt. The cycles of day and night continued on regardless. The rooks come each evening and leave each morning unaware of my presence or absence, they do not know of the images or insights that they inspired.

All seems the same.

And yet, looking closer, I see, pushing up through last year's brown leaves, delicate snowdrops, death and life coexisting.

The leaning tombstones of graves long forgotten lie outside a deconsecrated church, moss-covered, the hardness of stone made soft and green. This place of rest, these bodies, these bones have been abandoned by the Church and reclaimed by the forest: by moss and ivy, grass and briars, crow and fox.

The wild reclaims everything.

Even us.

Especially us.

Something is shifting in the world. The days are lengthening.

My days are soundtracked by crow calls. It seems they are everywhere, gathering sticks, building nests. Black-boned hedgerows are laced with frothy white blossom. A new cycle of life is being prepared for.

The birds are singing the song of new life as they herald the spring once more out of the bare branches of winter. They are the chorus that greet us as we emerge from the darkness of winter, calling forth the light. Life is breaking forth from its monochrome winter prison. Colour is returning in the yellow of daffodil and celandine, the pink of cherry blossom and the purple of crocus.

These are (still) times of wild revelation. It need not take apocalypse to remember. Another way of living in this world stands waiting. If only we could listen. If only we could remember. If only we could step into it and inhabit it. What will it take?

Here in the heart of the woods

The trees stand their ground.

The sun rises between them as it always has and always will.

And I am here.

Not the I that I was hoping to be, nor the I that I once was, but whoever or whatever I am now. I am here. Emerging. Remembering.

"I call my spirit back on the wings of crows. I call magic back on the wings of crows. I invite everyday magic and mysticism to enliven my days and it arrives on the wings of crows. I invite the Goddess to speak to and through me and she speaks with crows."

Molly Remer, *Walking with Persephone*

# Home Coming

Older, wiser, wilder. Transformed by the moon shadow in the white trees, the mud and the leaves, the eyes in the night, the screech owl and the sea, she rises.

She who has danced in the fire and not been burned,

She who has held the moon in her eye, birthed the world and lived to tell the tale.

She who has died and been reborn many times.

Here she stands, moon-streaked, wild-eyed.

No longer scared of the other worlds.

No longer afraid of the darkness.

She knows she belongs here.

And there.

That she can cross between them.

Eclipsed, occulted, reborn.

The woman of darkness who knows the power of flight.

Steps forward, places her cloak over her shoulders, picks up a stick, claims it to be a magic wand, and begins to beat the drum.

OOO

Feel the energy that you have pushed down all these years

All that you have bottled up, all that you have caged and clipped

Feel it in your belly, rising up with the spring

making the song of your heart come out of your mouth.

Hear your voice aloud.

Feel your wings stretch wide.

It is time.

(Finally, finally)

It is time.

OOO

In ancient days they read the skies.

Birds were omens

Heralding change.

These are ancient days.

We are remembering

The ways of the crow.

From north and south, east and west,

from sea and trees

From field and stream

We fly

Circling the moon,

Singing songs of silver,

In a world of tarnished gold.

Crow Moon rising

Shimmering bright

A new world woven

On our wings.

# Guidance

As you set out into the dark woods it is important to note that the literal danger of the dark woods is relative, depending on where in the world you live. In the modern Irish woods I walk through nothing can kill you bar a malicious human, or freak falling tree or lightning strike. Talking to US friends, the animals they share their forests with – bears, wolves, coyote, snakes and Lyme-infested ticks – add a much greater level of danger to any walk in the woods, day or night. Likewise wooded areas in and around cities can be no-go areas because of predatory men. But wherever we are, when we're in the wild, a primal sense of fear kicks in, especially when we are far from home, alone and lost. This is the journey of the dark woods.

With that in mind, I wanted to share few words of guidance before you set out for the heart of the forest. (Inside/outside).

1.  Do not attempt to enter the dark heart of the woods alone without first knowing the surrounding area. You'll need to circle it many, many times looking, listening, get to know the terrain intimately.

2.  Ensure you are well resourced. Have sturdy footwear. Food and drink. Suitable clothes. Take a map, trust local knowledge more… and be prepared to adapt to what you find.

3.  Keep your eyes and ears open. Follow the signs: the hop of a bird, the scurry of a squirrel, a change in the breeze, the darkening of the sky. Look out for tracks. Animal tracks, dog, wolf bear, human… These are clues.

4.  Beware of briars, poison ivy and nettles.

5.  Look out for tools. Practical tools, magical tools.

6.  Keep your eyes open for the sacred grove, the clearing in the midst of the forest where light penetrates the dark, where fairies gather. Stop rest, say your prayers. Touch a tree. Give thanks. Lie your body down on the ground and be held. Sing, dance, listen.

7.  Always remember your way out may not be the way in.

8.  Write and tell stories about your adventures in the woods. Humans have done it for as long as they have existed. We turn the woods into words: trees into paper, paper into books. The books feed more minds. Create more guidebooks. For humans to go and encounter the woods generation after generation. With stories of warnings, adventures and initiations. Just like this.

# Author's Note

I have traveled through many initiations consciously and unconsciously on my way here. Under the light of many moons – reaching for the moon, moon time, honeymoon, babymoon – each corresponding to an archetype born within me. The initiation to motherhood and the emergence of the Creative Rainbow Mother archetype. The initiation to being an author and publisher getting my creative work out into the world. The journey of *Burning Woman,* the initiation of Fire, of finding my authentic voice, putting my power out into the world and being burnt. The initiation of the bodymind of illness and the discovery of my neurodivergence in *Medicine Woman.* The reconnection with the roots of my creative self through the Creatrix archetype. The initiation of Water through *She of the Sea.* And now, I find myself here. A double initiation, of Earth and Air, mushroom and crow. An integration of all I have learned, the embodiment of these knowings.

An initiation into my wild woman self, the strangest and hardest yet: *Crow Moon.*

Everything you read in the pages of this book is true. Either to my surface self…or my soul self. Often to both. It is, as I have learned to say, "magical and real: both".

The experiences that I share in this book felt strange, inexplicable and momentous from the inside…and yet to the outside world what was to be seen? A two-year stretch of intense chronic migraines often half the days of each month; a flourishing of image-making, illustrating *Crow Moon, The Kitchen Witch Companion, Soulful Pregnancy* and the cover art for the new edition of *Moon Time;* an increased number of walks in the woods and a burgeoning of new special interests in corvids and fungi. All of this collided and interwove within to make sense of symbols, images and experiences that had recurred throughout my life but had no obvious through thread.

First came the crows. Then the mushrooms. (As those who follow my social media accounts can attest, there were lots and lots of mushroom pictures!) *Crow Moon* was a long and tortuous initiation – through real world encounters with mushrooms, crows and the woods, as well as strange synchronicities, dreams, trance, therapeutic work and art making – in strange, fractured parts. Later came the insight through research. This has always been the way for me: reading and writing as a way of understanding what has just happened to me.

This book is an attempt to recreate the experience of initiation, a shift in consciousness, through word and image…with the desire to instigate it in the reader. I have never seen this done before. I don't know if it can be. But that is my intention. I have been true to the process, to capturing it in simple words and striking images. In moving between poetry and process, breaking down paragraphs and allowing words to be freed from traditional structures. In doing so my intention is to free the potency of word as symbol. Taking the text from out of the mental sphere into the imaginative realm, making the reading of it experiential rather than intellectual.

The book was written in many innovative ways – dictation whilst walking the woods and working in darkened rooms on large sheets of paper in charcoal and Sharpie, moving from word to image and back again.

I was fascinated to discover powerful symbolic images of initiation working on me in the midst of my own pretty average modern life of driving the kids to school, watching Netflix, cooking dinner and unblocking the sink. What always amazes me is that the images which emerge are often ones that have fascinated our species for millennia: in religions and spiritual practices, depth psychology, art… It would freak me out far less if I didn't find the rich history of symbology backing up real world experiences that I had just had.

I must emphasise that it is not my specialness I am trying to assert when I write of these experiences. In fact, just the opposite. It is the ubiquity of them. The ever-present mysteries of the depths which have revealed themselves to humans since the dawn of our cultures is still here. Rich and alive. The collective unconscious is available to all of us outside of the therapy room or high-priced initiatory retreats. They are democratic and ever-present, connecting all of us who allow space, time and courage for a deeper awareness of the life process within us. The reason we do not know this is that we are encouraged not to speak of such things for fear of others thinking we are crazy. And so, we keep them to ourselves, trying instead to see the world as we have always been told it was.

The messengers of the wild and sacred are imprinted on every layer of our beings and the world around us waiting, patiently, to be seen, to be recognised, to lead us back to ourselves, the earth, the sacred and each other.

It is time.

# About the Author

Lucy H. Pearce is driven by a need to create, connect and inspire. A best-selling author, vibrant artist, respected publisher and editor, her work focuses on self-knowledge and healing through creativity, archetypes and cyclical living. She gives voice to the soul: the spiritual, the liminal, the darkness and discomfort and the magical in the midst of the mundane. Often described as raw, authentic and life-changing, her work encourages authentic paths to self-expression and is celebrated particularly by highly sensitive and neurodivergent women.

With a degree in History of Ideas and English Literature from Kingston University, and a graduate degree in teaching English and Drama from Cambridge – words, ideas and their free expression lie at the heart of her work. She has taught through the arts for nearly twenty years, in schools, private classes and online.

Her many books include Nautilus Silver Award winners – *Creatrix: she who makes; Medicine Woman; Burning Woman* and #1 Amazon bestsellers *Moon Time* and *The Rainbow Way*.

Lucy is the founder and creative director of Womancraft Publishing, established in 2014, which publishes life-changing, paradigm-shifting books by women, for women.

She is the mother of three children and lives on the south coast of Ireland.

Lucyhpearce.com  
Womancraftpublishing.com

Instagram @lucyhpearce  
Facebook @dreamingaloudnt

# Artist Statement

"Bypassing the intellect, often inaccessible to conscious thought, these multidimensional images strike to the heart of awareness. They vibrate within our psyches, oscillating between various levels of meaning. They are the unconscious source of our thoughts and emotions... As we are drawn deeper into each form and expression of the archetype, we begin to assimilate the primordial energy that creates it."

Layne Redmond, *When the Drummers Were Women*

You cannot do initiation with your mind. It does not make sense. It is a process of the soul. This is where the images come in. They are our soul language.

The process of this book centred on and was guided by image-making. The images themselves showed the steps on the psychological journey of entering the dark woods, of transformation.

I committed to following these images wherever they took me, however they needed to be expressed. However strange or messy or repetitive that might be. My allegiance was to the images. Even when they scared me.

In *Crow Moon,* I broke the only rule my A-Level art teacher ever gave me: don't use black, because black is not a colour. Working in black is something I was taught never to do. These images demanded to be black and white. Black crow, white moon. Yin and yang.

As a neurodivergent person I am often accused of having black and white thinking about things – I decided to harness this propensity in these images, to see where it would take me if I saw it as a gift, rather than a deficit.

And so, I began following the narrative and symbology as it revealed itself, witnessing as it emerged in awe. This is how I have always most loved art. Using creative imagination and the power of symbol and nature to slip the bonds of patriarchal culture and definitions of what it is to be a woman. Embracing the power of shapeshifting. A different way of seeing ourselves and our world, a shift in perception.

"It's through emergent images that the soul moves life force around inside of us. Additional interactions with what we hope will be a life-giving image will help the energy move along more swiftly, more fully than would happen otherwise."

This Jungian Life, "Creative Depression"

Since my teens I have had a passion for the work of both Symbolist and Surrealist artists and the work of Carl Jung. Surrealism centres the absurd, sharing the incongruous alongside the mundane, juxtaposing the two in a way that both jars and yet seems achingly possible. It has been an approach I have loved since my teens. One that connects images not through meaning but through form, to discover new ways of thinking and being.

The Surrealists took the emergent tools of psychotherapy – namely free association of images from both dream and waking imagination – in order to access the contents of the unconscious. This is the technique I used for this book.

The first of the images in the book came through to me on the night before Halloween. We had been to a lantern parade through a local woods, led by drummers, who I only spotted at the end were wearing crow masks. I wore my black cape for the first time in public. It felt like many threads were tied together that evening. The image came through in the dark, fast, emergent and insistent, I would not be let sleep until it was captured. A hooded figure, turned to the side, a crow's beak. It emerged in graphic black and white. It looked different to anything I had made before. It intrigued me... the character, the style. I wanted to know more.

I let the intriguing image sit for a couple of weeks. Then the images started pouring through during a ten-day migraine. Painful but profound, it felt like an awakening into another level of my visioning self.

I was stuck in a darkened room, unable to see the end of autumn in the woods, unable to do my daily visit to the mushrooms and trees. Instead, I was living it internally, experiencing the connections visually and spiritually. The hooded figure emerged again. She became a slow-motion comic strip, as each image appeared, first her cloaked back to me, then turning, then revealing her face, then fully transforming into Bird Woman. She was both me... and not me. Each image was not

194

planned but channeled, sometimes a snapshot vision appeared to me before I started, but more often it emerged as I began to draw, revealing itself to me as amazed bystander.

I followed the images into the unknown, to see what my unconscious mind would throw up… many times I didn't like where the journey was taking me. For a long time, I refused the images that came up. I wanted them to have a different meaning, a different insight. I wanted the book to reach a different conclusion. I didn't want it to be so personal… and yet, here it was.

I had been playing with creating branches and feathers for years in many different media. I had been drawing realistic branches on the iPad for the past couple of weeks, as well as crows in ink, charcoal, watercolour and finally digitally. All these came together in the artwork for the book, once I had been gifted the style.

Each image started in the same way… a ritual creation of sacred space: first the black square, then a white full moon circle. This form was a vital container. A staging ground. Then the images emerged.

"In modern art the square and circle appear but separate. In the past these two abstract figures (the circle and square) would have been united, and would have expressed a world of thoughts and feelings… The circle is symbol of the psyche… The square… is a symbol of earthbound matter. The symbolic alchemical concept of the squared circle – a symbol of wholeness and union of opposites."

Aniela Jaffé, *Man and his Symbols*

To me the square and circle, black and white, crow and moon is a balancing of energetics, representing masculine and feminine, yin and yang. It was an intuitive decision that became the framework for all the images in the book. I made the decision to bring the yin yang principal to these basic shapes: the squares do not have straight but organic wavy edges, the circles are not organic but geometric, altered by technology from a shaky hand-drawn line. The circle represents a visual focus, a lens or spotlight for illumination of the subject. Where objects pass outside of the lens, their meanings and definition are reversed. The white circle is the moon. Moonlight illuminates in a different way with high contrast white light and shadow, bringing out strange dimensions, something that the migraine does.

For Jung drawing circles was a wholing, healing act for the psyche. I most definitely found it to be so. Creating the images was both exhilarating and deeply soothing, helping me to see more deeply into the material that was emerging in my psyche, allowing to give form to the feelings that was less personal, diffusing the emotional charge, helping me to understand my journey symbolically.

I knew the images were an integral part of this book, that they were to be a way to work with and develop more deeply the WORD + image process that I had been using and teaching for several years. This too was an immense gift, and one that fed into both my teaching and a forthcoming book on the subject.

The images also reflected the experience of migraine... branches and roots were also the blood vessels I could see illuminated in my migrainous eye, was also the flash of illumination in the form of lightning, symbol of inspiration and transformation. The moon was the orb of light that my pupil becomes in migraine, the stark black and white patterns, almost psychedelic, seemed to connect the experience of migraine and the patterns people talk of being produced by hallucinogenic mushrooms. It was an exploration of what is hidden and what is revealed: an exploration of non-rational vision and altered consciousness.

"Symbols are natural attempts to reconcile and
reunite opposites within the psyche."

C.G. Jung, *Man and his Symbols*

The images speak of the transformation of the binary – crow: black, moon: white, but black becoming white where it crosses a boundary, turning reality inside out, shifting our perception, our understanding of the solidity of the known world, illuminating the unexpected, asking us to look again, to see differently, to shift our learned presumptions and travel consciously into the unknown. These images invite us to linger in the strangeness, to look more closely, to stay rooted in this other reality through shape and pattern, opening to the connections that we usually discount with our logical minds. These images initiate us into other ways of seeing: seeing into, seeing through, seeing god in the gaps, awe in the interplay of light and dark. They allow us to experience and remember the paradoxical contrasts that lie at the very heart of life.

# Contributors

## Imelda Almqvist

Imelda Almqvist is a painter, forest witch, author of eight books and international teacher of Sacred Art and Seiðr. She appears in a TV program, titled "Ice Age Shaman", made for the Smithsonian Museum (Mystic Britain). Pregnant Hag Teachings is her online school.
shaman-healer-painter.co.uk

## Holly Baker

Holly lives in the Lake District with her family, having moved from London. The landscape has re-ignited her creativity in the last few years. Alongside running a small eco shop she writes poetry and plays music. More writing can be found on Instagram: @whatyourmotherdidnttellyou

## Kelley Davis Sookram

Kelley is a nature loving girl, passionate about creating and finding inspiration through authentic interactions with others. Fostering sacred moments, empowering others, and tapping into Divine connection brings her joy. She considers herself a lifelong learner in this experience she calls Earth school and is forever grateful for the company along the way. Instagram: @leavingclouddesigns

## Megan Desrosiers

Megan is a mystical being who believes that challenges and traumas hold the keys to personal transformation. Through her art, writing, ritual, and healing practices, she supports others in their healing journeys and inspires them to become more comfortable with the continuous cycles of life and death. You can learn more about her work at herbalbonesart.com

## Gemma Clark and Isabel Brady

An Earth loving feminist campaigner and teacher from Scotland and her mother.
Twitter @Gemma_clark14 / TikTok @Gemma_clark1

## Chloe Elgar

Chloe Elgar is a Rune Witch and a Seer. She is the one who sees with her eyes closed. Chloe's work is rooted in the traditions of the North, guided by the Runes, the wild, and her ancestors. She is the author of the popular psychic memoir, *Revealed by Darkness,* and the creator of the e-commerce shop, Night Wing Goods. channeledbychloe.com / Instagram @channeledbychloe

## Susie Quatermass

Susie Quatermass, artist, sculptress, Goddess loving Priestess of Avalon based in Glastonbury UK. Creatrix at Goddess Temple Gifts, Ceremonial Priestess at Glastonbury Goddess Temple. Anasryma activist and Sheela na Gig Sister.
Instagram: @susiequatermass / Email: Susiequatermass@gmail.com for info on courses and activism.

## Hazel Evans MA

Mentor, visionary artist, writer and ceremonialist, Hazel is an award-winning artist and a medicine woman with a powerful journey of reclaiming her shamanic roots, becoming a priestess of sacred sexuality, and surviving narcissistic abuse. She is a profound leader and mentor of deep feminine wisdom, creation, and consciousness. hazelevans.co.uk

## Enagh Farrell

Enagh Farrell is an illustrator living in Dublin. She is interested in our connection to the natural world and exploring ways in which we might reconnect. Her work is inspired by mythology and stories that establish a connectivity between the ecology, spirit, and history of place.
Website: enaghfarrell.com

## Raven S Hunter

Raven S Hunter is an artist, songwriter, astrologer and writer living in the mountains of New Mexico, Land of Enchantment. Raven weaves nature's beauty and the sacred feminine into her art, music and writing. Samples of her work can be seen on her Facebook page using her mundane name, Peg Edmister. Email: ravendreams55@yahoo.com

## Kimberley Jones

Multi-award-winning Soul Midwife, Sacred Feminist and Medicine Woman, Kimberley Jones has been helping women all over the world for twenty-five years to heal the witch wound, reclaim their power and remember their magic. Kimberley is a deep seer and wise woman sharing teachings, transmissions, Tarot and art and is currently studying for a PhD on intergenerational trauma and ancestral healing. kimberleyjones.co.uk

## Eva Lake

Eva Lake is a long-standing TV storyliner who was guided by life and circumstance, to follow a very different path. Now a reiki master teacher, ceremonialist and end of life doula, Eva works in the area of death positivity and awareness. She also holds space for people as they journey through their various life transitions. evalake.co.uk

## Rebecca Lowe

Rebecca Lowe is a freelance writer, poet, mother, and organiser of spoken word events from Swansea, South Wales. Her first poetry collection *Blood and Water* was published by The Seventh Quarry Press in 2020. She is a lover of music, creativity, folklore and nature. Links to her poetry and music can be found on YouTube @Becky Lowe Swansea / Twitter @BeckyLowePoet

## Janet Lucy

Janet Lucy is the co-author of *Moon Mother, Moon Daughter – Myths and Rituals that Celebrate a Girl's Coming of Age; Moon Mother, Moon Daughter Moon Circles Facilitator's Guide* and *By the Light of the Moon* journal; and three award-winning children's books, *Makana is a Gift, Mermaid Dreams,* and *The Three Sunflowers.* She lives in Santa Barbara, California. janetlucyink.com

## Kirstin McCulloch

Kirstin McCulloch brings a little bit of whimsy into the world with beautiful multi-layered, mixed-media artworks, featuring mainly big-eyed characters, who have intricate stories hidden in the paintings. Located on Wiradjuri country, NSW Australia, she draws inspiration for her paintings and her collection of whimsical treasures, from her girls and the ever-changing landscapes and seasons surrounding her. Instagram: @lillibeandesigns

## Barbara O'Meara

Barbara O'Meara, BA (Hons) Fine Art Painting and H.Dip Community Arts Education NCAD, is a professional visual artist, art activist and educator, published writer and illustrator. She co-edited *Soul Seers: an Irish Anthology of Celtic Shamanism* featuring her artwork and has had twenty-two nationwide solo exhibitions to date. Her community arts work includes Women's Collective Ireland. She is continually developing empowering women's 'Art as Activism' projects. barbaraomearaartist.com

## Polly Paton Brown

Polly Paton-Brown is an artist, writer and dollmaker living in Shropshire with her partner and menagerie of animals, including dogs, cats, horses and sheep. A former trauma therapist, Polly now spends her time helping people connect with the sacred through creativity and nature. Her passion is helping those who have been wounded by organised religion of any sort.
Website: pollypatonbrownartist.com
Facebook: Polly Paton-Brown: Doll-Lady, Artist and Sacred Scribe

## Cindy Read

Cindy is a mixed media and fiber artist who lives in the state of Maine on the original homeland of the Penobscot Nation. What comes from her heart and mind through her hands is dedicated to healing for the earth and for all living beings.

## Linda Ruff

Linda is a counsellor, circle holder and death doula who lives on the sacred lands of the Wurrundjeri people in suburban Melbourne, Australia. She works with women through their rites of passage walking beside us as we weave ourselves back into wild landscapes and community.
Website: wovenincounselling.com

## Christina Swan-Doyle

A moon lover inspired by Nature. Happiest when sitting on a beach, close to the waves or delving deep into the forest surrounded by trees. Instagram/Facebook: @Serenity Natural Therapies

## Nicola Wood

Nicola holds women circles as part of her offering at Women Replanting. She's also a creative, enjoying writing, poetry, painting and singing. She co-founded a local charity in 2016 working with people in the UK asylum system and presently still works within the charity sector supporting unpaid carers. Nicola lives in Wiltshire with her three kids and husband. Instagram: @womenreplanting

# Acknowledgements

Thank you to Molly Remer and Sarah Robinson for your journeys in the wild woods that came before and after mine.

To Patrick for listening when I needed to untangle the story of the book, and keeping our life running whilst I was stuck in a dark room.

Thank you to my early readers – Gina Martin, Ariele Myers, Cat Hawkins, Awen Clement, Judith Laxer, Sarah Robinson and Mary Lunnen for their insights and enthusiasm.

Thank you to all the women who heard the call and contributed their experiences and insights into Crow and Bird Woman. There was not space to print them all, but I am so grateful to you for sharing your knowings with me and reminding me that I am not alone.

Alexandra de Angelis

Angela Bigler

Barbara O'Meara

Chloe Elgar

Christina Swan-Doyle

Cindy Read

Denise Gushue

Enagh Farrell

Ellie Peckham Paterson

Elyse Welles

Eva Lake

Gemma Clark

Hazel Evans

Holly Baker

Imelda Almqvist

Kathy Curran

Kelley Davis Sookram

Kimberley Jones

Kirstin McCulloch

Janet Lucy

Jules Swindel

Linda Ruff

Liz Wahba

Megan Desrosiers

Michalu

Nicola Wood

Polly Patton Brown

Raven S Hunter

Ravina Shive

Rebecca Kimberly

Rebecca Lowe

Reva Adie

Susie Quatermass

Suzanna

Tanya Levy

Tayria Ward

# Bibliography

*Sacred Symbols: Peoples, Religions, Mysteries* – Robert Adkinson (ed.)

*Art is a Spiritual Path: Engaging the Sacred through the Practice of Art and Writing* – Pat B. Allen

*Art is a Way of Knowing: A Guide to Self-Knowledge and Spiritual Fulfillment Through Creativity* – Pat B. Allen

*The Book of Symbols* – ARAS

*1001 Ideas That Changed the Way We Think* – Robert Arp

*Phosphorescence: On awe, wonder and things that sustain you when the world goes dark* – Julia Baird

*The Myth of the Goddess: Evolution of an Image* – Anne Baring and Jules Cashford

*If Women Rose Rooted: A Life-Changing Journey to Authenticity and Belonging* – Sharon Blackie

*The Enchanted Life: Reclaiming the Magic and Wisdom of the Natural World* – Sharon Blackie

*Women Artists and the Surrealist Movement* – Whitney Chadwick

*On Psychotherapy* – Petrushka Clarkson

*Crow Country* – Mark Cocker

*Crow Mother and the Dog God* – Meinrad Craighead

*An Illustrated Encyclopedia of Traditional Symbols* – J.C. Cooper

*An Irish Atlantic Rainforest: A Personal Journey into the Magic of Rewilding* – Eoghan Daltun

*The Holy Wild: A Heathen Bible for the Untamed Woman* – Danielle Dulsky

*The Blue Jay's Dance: A Memoir of Early Motherhood* – Louise Erdrich

*Women Who Run with the Wolves* – Clarissa Pinkola Estés

*Initiated: Memoir of a Witch* – Amanda Yates Garcia

*The Living Goddesses* – Marija Gimbutas

*Apocalyptic Witchcraft* – Peter Grey

*Waking the Witch* – Pam Grossman

*Witchcraft: the library of esoterica* – Jessica Hundley and Pam Grossman (eds.)

*The Doors of Perception* – Aldous Huxley

*Shape Shifters: shaman women in contemporary society* – Michelle Jamal

*Seeing Through the World: Jean Gebser and Integral Consciousness* – Jeremy Johnson

*The Red Book* – C.G. Jung

*The Archetypes and the Collective Unconscious* – C.G. Jung

*Symbols of Transformation* – C.G. Jung

*Memories, Dreams, Reflections* – C.G. Jung

*Man and his Symbols* – C.G. Jung

*The Wild Unknown Archetypes Guidebook* – Kim Krans

*The Wheel: A Witch's Path Back to the Ancient Self* – Jennifer Lane

*The Sister from Below: When the Muse Gets Her Way* – Naomi Ruth Lowinsky

*Underland* – Robert MacFarlane

*Tree Dogs, Banshee Fingers* – Manchán Magan

*Thirty-Two Words for Field* – Manchán Magan

*Gifts of the Crows* – John M. Marzluff and Tony Angell

*In the Company of Crows and Ravens* – John M. Marzluff and Tony Angell

*Seasons of the Witch* – Patricia Monaghan

*Not in His Image* – John Lamb Nash

*Wild* – Amy Jeffs

*Burning Woman* – Lucy H. Pearce

*Creatrix: she who makes* – Lucy H. Pearce

*Medicine Woman: reclaiming the soul of healing* – Lucy H. Pearce

*She of the Sea* – Lucy H. Pearce

*When the Drummers Were Women: a spiritual history of rhythm* – Layne Redmond

*Walking with Persephone: a journey of midlife descent and renewal* – Molly Remer

*A Wild Soul Woman: 5 Earth Archetypes to Unleash Your Full Feminine Power* – Mary Reynolds Thomson

*The Book of the Raven: corvids in art and legend* – Caroline Roberts and Agnes Hyland

*Kitchen Witch: food, folklore, fairy tale* – Sarah Robinson

*The Kitchen Witch Companion: Recipes, Rituals & Reflections* – Sarah Robinson and Lucy H. Pearce

*Witchbody* – Sabrina Scott

*Entangled Lives* – Merlin Sheldrake

*Finding the Mother Tree: Discovering the Wisdom of the Forest* – Suzanne Simard

*Return of the dark/light mother or New Age Armageddon?* – Monica Sjöö

*The Shadow King: the invisible force that holds women back* – Sidra Stone

*A Spell in the Wild: A Year (and Six Centuries) of Magic* – Alice Tarbuck

*The Witch and the Clown: two archetypes of human sexuality* – Ann and Barry Ulanov

*Changeling* – Adrian Wachter

*The Woman's Dictionary of Symbols* – Barbara G. Walker

*The Woman's Encyclopedia of Myths and Secrets* – Barbara G. Walker

The Three Marriages – David Whyte
Pregnant Darkness: alchemy and the rebirth of consciousness – Monika Wikman
When Women Were Birds: fifty-four variations on voice – Terry Tempest Williams

# Art

The Diary of Frida Kahlo
Crow Tarot – M. J. Cullinane
The Art of the Occult: a visual sourcebook for the modern mystic – S. Elizabeth
Blossom and Bones – Kim Krans
The Wild Unknown Archetypes – Kim Krans
Draw Yourself Calm: Draw Slow, Stress Less – Amy Maricle
Raven Girl – Audrey Niffenegger
Migraine Art: The Migraine Experience from Within – Klaus Podoll, Derek Robinson, et al.
Bridget Riley
Witchbody – Sabrina Scott
The Arrival – Shaun Tan
Li – David Wade

# Poetry

Terrapin: Poems by Wendell Berry – Wendell Berry
Selected Poems – Emily Dickinson
Crow: From the Life and Songs of the Crow – Ted Hughes
Bird-Woman – Em Strang
The Bell and the Blackbird – David Whyte
Pilgrim – David Whyte

# Fiction

*I Know Why the Caged Bird Sings* – Maya Angelou
*A Pinch of Magic* – Michelle Harrison
*The Once and Future Witches* – Alix E. Harrow
*The Rules of Magic* – Alice Hoffman
*Grief is the Thing with Feathers* – Max Porter
*The Vile Village (A Series of Unfortunate Events, Book 7)* – Lemony Snickett

# Podcasts

This Jungian Life episodes:
  7 – Hearing Voices
  10 – Synchronicity
  11 – Fairy Tales
  13 – Active Imagination
  18 – Creative Depression
  25 – The Psychology of Divination
  27 – Dream Animals
  186 – The Archetype of the Witch
The Revelation Project Podcast with Monica Rodgers – Sophie Strand episode
Missing Witches:
  Sarah Gottesdiener: Witchcraft 1011 and Taking Our Own Advice
  Terry Tempest William – A Pencil is a Wand is a Weapon
  Margaret Murray: What Science Calls Nature and Religion Calls God
  Maria Sabina: "I am the Woman Who Shepherds the Immense."
  Pixie Coleman Smith – "Look for the Door into the Unknown Country"
  Monica Sjoo: "The Earth is a Witch and the Men Still Burn Her"
Short Cuts. Leonora Carrington
In Our Time: Surrealism – BBC 4
London Drawing Group classes:
  Queer Mycologies
  A Feminist Guide to Fungi
Spirit Box – Adrian Wachter: Changeling

# Online Resources

"Mythic Guidance for Times When We are Lost in the Dark Forest" – Reverend Dr Sushmita Mukherjee,
  on-seeing.com/home/2019/6/24/mythic-guidance-for-times-when-we-are-lost-in-the-dark-forest
"The Spiritual Meaning of Crows" – Lauren David, mindbodygreen.com/articles/crow-symbolism
"Rewilding Witchcraft" – Peter Grey, scarletimprint.com/journal/rewilding-witchcraft

# Endnotes

1 theguardian.com/environment/2020/apr/27/the-bliss-of-a-quiet-period-lockdown-is-a-unique-chance-to-study-the-nature-of-cities-aoe

2 John M. Marzluff and Tony Angell, *In the Company of Crows and Ravens*

3 John M. Marzluff and Tony Angell, *Gifts of the Crows*

4 thetimes.co.uk/article/ice-age-left-its-mark-on-divided-crows

5 arranbirding.co.uk/hooded-and-carrion-crows.html

6 "By soul I mean the invisible, innate beingness of each of us beyond our physical human bodies. The ancient Greeks used the term psyche to express "the soul, mind, spirit; breath; life, one's life, the animating principle or entity which occupies and directs the physical body." But for many today the term psyche brings to mind the modern usage by our medical fields, where it is really just a synonym for mind and usually associated with mental health, or rather, mental illness. [...] I have chosen to stick with soul which, for me, retains the sense of the myriad untouchable energies of being far beyond just the mental. I am fully aware that some folks struggle with this term. In our modern, Western scientific and materialist context, soul is not considered a real thing. There is no diagram for it in our biology textbooks, no chemical equation. You cannot prove soul. And yet, you know it, you sense it, when it is present, and when it is absent." From my book *Creatrix*

7 When Crow is capitalised, it refers to Crow as symbol or archetype.

8 theguardian.com/uk-news/2021/jan/14/tower-of-london-raven-missing-feared-dead

9 gatecottages.wordpress.com/2011/04/05/rostellan-castlehouse

10 Bruno Bettelheim, *The Uses of Enchantment: The Meaning and Importance of Fairy Tales*

11 on-seeing.com/home/2019/6/24/mythic-guidance-for-times-when-we-are-lost-in-the-dark-forest

12 M. L von Franz, "The Process of Individualation" in *Man and his Symbols*

13 Wikipedia Metanoia wikipedia.org/wiki/Metanoia_(psychology)

14 Robert Arp, *1001 Ideas That Changed the Way We Think*

15 Petrushka Clarkson, *On Psychotherapy*

16 on-seeing.com/home/2019/6/24/mythic-guidance-for-times-when-we-are-lost-in-the-dark-forest

17 J.C. Cooper, *An Illustrated Encyclopedia of Traditional Symbols*

18 Anne Baring and Jules Cashford, *The Myth of the Goddess: Evolution of an Image*

19 Marija Gimbutas, *The Living Goddesses*

20 Maria Sabina: "I am the Woman who Shepherds the Immense" – Missing Witches podcast.

21 Jeremy Johnson, *Seeing Through the World: Jean Gebser and Integral Consciousness*

22 culture.pl/en/article/the-extraordinary-life-of-simona-kossak

# About Womancraft

Womancraft Publishing was founded on the revolutionary vision that women and words can change the world. We act as midwife to transformational women's words that have the power to challenge, inspire, heal and speak to the silenced aspects of ourselves, empowering our readers to actively co-create cultures that value and support the female and feminine. Our books have been #1 Amazon bestsellers in many categories, as well as Nautilus and Women's Spirituality Award winners.

As we find ourselves in a time where old stories, old answers and ways of being are losing their authority and relevance, we at Womancraft are actively looking for new ways forward. Our books ask important questions. We aim to share a diverse range of voices, of different ages, backgrounds, sexual orientations and neurotypes, seeking every greater diversity, whilst acknowledging our limitations as a small press.

Whilst far from perfect, we are proud that in our small way, Womancraft is walking its talk, living the new paradigm in the crumbling heart of the old: through financially empowering creative people, through words that honour the Feminine, through healthy working practices, and through integrating business with our lives, and rooting our economic decisions in what supports and sustains our natural environment. We are learning and improving all the time. I hope that one day soon, what we do is seen as nothing remarkable, just the norm.

We work on a full circle model of giving and receiving: reaching backwards, supporting Treesisters' reforestation projects and the UNHCR girls' education fund, and forwards via Worldreader, providing e-books at no-cost to education projects for girls and women in developing countries. We donate many paperback copies to education projects and women's libraries around the world. We speak from our place within the circle of women, sharing our vision, and encouraging them to share it onwards, in ever-widening circles.

We are honoured that the Womancraft community is growing internationally year on year, seeding red tents, book groups, women's circles, ceremonies and classes into the fabric of our world. Join the revolution! Sign up to the mailing list at womancraftpublishing.com and find us on social media for exclusive offers:

 womancraftpublishing

 womancraft_publishing

**Signed copies of all titles available from**
**womancraftpublishing.com**

# Use of Womancraft Work

Often women contact us asking if and how they may use our work. We love seeing our work out in the world. We love you sharing our words further. And we ask that you respect our hard work by acknowledging the source of the words.

We are delighted for short quotes from our books – up to 200 words – to be shared as memes or in your own articles or books, provided they are clearly accompanied by the author's name and the book's title.

We are also very happy for the materials in our books to be shared amongst women's communities: to be studied by book groups, discussed in classes, read from in ceremony, quoted on social media… with the following provisos:

☾ If content from the book is shared in written or spoken form, the book's author and title must be referenced clearly.

☾ The only person fully qualified to teach the material from any of our titles is the author of the book itself. There are no accredited teachers of this work. Please do not make claims of this sort.

☾ If you are creating a course devoted to the content of one of our books, its title and author must be clearly acknowledged on all promotional material (posters, websites, social media posts).

☾ The book's cover may be used in promotional materials or social media posts. The cover art is copyright of the artist and has been licensed exclusively for this book. Any element of the book's cover or font may not be used in branding your own marketing materials when teaching the content of the book, or content very similar to the original book.

☾ No more than two double page spreads, or four single pages of any book may be photocopied as teaching materials.

We are delighted to offer a 20% discount of over five copies going to one address. You can order these on our webshop, or email us. If you require further clarification, email us at: info@womancraftpublishing.com

# Burning Woman

## Lucy H. Pearce

*Burning Woman* is a breath-taking and controversial woman's journey through history – personal and cultural – on a quest to find and free her own power.

Uncompromising and all-encompassing, Lucy H. Pearce uncovers the archetype of the Burning Women of days gone by – Joan of Arc and the witch trials, through to the way women are burned today in cyber bullying, acid attacks, shaming and burnout, fearlessly examining the roots of Feminine power – what it is, how it has been controlled, and why it needs to be unleashed on the world during our modern Burning Times.

*Burning Woman* explores:

☾ Burning from within: a woman's power – how to build it, engage it and not be destroyed by it.

☾ Burning from without: the role of shame, and honour in the time-worn ways the dominant culture uses fire to control the Feminine.

☾ The darkness: overcoming our fear of the dark, and discovering its importance in cultivating power.

This incendiary text was written for women who burn with passion, have been burned with shame, and who at another time, in another place, would have been burned at the stake. With contributions from leading burning women of our era: Isabel Abbott, ALisa Starkweather, Shiloh Sophia McCloud, Molly Remer, Julie Daley, Bethany Webster…

# Walking with Persephone:
## A Journey of Midlife Descent and Renewal

### Molly Remer

Midlife can be a time of great change – inner and outer: a time of letting go of the old, burnout and disillusionment. But how do we journey through this? And what can we learn in the process? Molly Remer is our personal guide to the unraveling and reweaving required in midlife. She invites you to take a walk with the goddess Persephone, whose story of descent into the underworld has much to teach us.

*Walking with Persephone* is a story of devotion and renewal that weaves together personal experiences, insights, observations, and reflections with experiences in practical priestessing, family life, and explorations of the natural world. It advocates opening our eyes to the wonder around us, encouraging the reader to both look within themselves for truths about living, but also to the earth, the air, the sky, the animals, and plants.

# She of the Sea

### Lucy H. Pearce

A lyrical exploration of the call of the sea and the depth of our connection to it, rooted in the author's personal experience living on the coast of the Celtic Sea, in Ireland.

This book spans from coastal plants to the colour blue, pebbles to prayer, via shapeshifting and suicidal ideation, erosion and immersion, cold water swimming and water birth, seaweed and cyanotypes, from Japanese freedivers and Celtic sea goddesses, selkies to surfing, and mermaids to Mary.

*She of the Sea* is a strange and wonderful deep dive into the inner sea and the Feminine, exploring where the real and the magical, the salty and the sacred meet, within and without, and what implications this has for us as both individuals... and a species in these tumultuous times.

# The Witch and the Wildwood

## Sarah Robinson

Welcome to the wildwood, where magic hides in ancient roots.

In the hidden shadows amongst the tree, tales of witches are whispered. What is it about these figures that has captured our imaginations for so long? What is it that draws us to the dark, tangled heart of the woods?

In this book, we will delve into stories of the woods as told through some of its most enchanting inhabitants; witches, fairy folk and magical creatures.

Stories rooted in folklore and legend reflect our desires to understand and explore the unknown. By delving into these tales, we can gain insight into our own relationship with nature, power, and perhaps even discover new ways of connecting with the world around us. This is an invitation to find enchantment in woodland and wild places. To delight in myth, magic and nature, forgotten superstitions, rituals and celebrations. And why not? Surely, we can all bear a little more magic, and a little more wild in our days.

So, let's journey through the bewitching folklore of the woods, and be prepared to fall under the enchantment of the witch maidens, deer-women, she-wolves, 'wildalones' and women of wild waters who sit in willow trees plotting revenge...